Revivalism

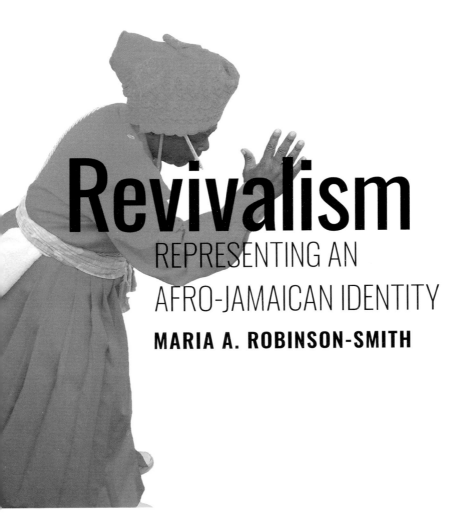

Revivalism

REPRESENTING AN
AFRO-JAMAICAN IDENTITY

MARIA A. ROBINSON-SMITH

The University of the West Indies Press
Jamaica • Barbados • Trinidad and Tobago

The University of the West Indies Press
7A Gibraltar Hall Road, Mona
Kingston 7, Jamaica
www.uwipress.com

A catalogue record of this book is available from the
National Library of Jamaica.

ISBN: 978-976-640-654-7 (print)
978-976-640-655-4 (Kindle)
978-976-640-656-1 (ePub)

Cover photograph by Clinton Hutton
Book and cover design by Robert Harris
Set in Minion Pro 11/15 x 24
Printed in the United States of America

Published with support from the Culture, Health, Arts, Sports and
Education (CHASE) Fund.

TO THE MEMORY OF MY LATE HUSBAND,
FRANKLYN LEROY SMITH,
AND THE MEMORY OF MY ANCESTORS

Contents

Illustrations

Photographs by the author unless otherwise credited.

Maps

List of Sites

Site 1.   Zion Sacred Heart of Christ Sabbath Church, Holt Close
Site 2.   St Michaels
Site 3.   Gethsemane United Holy Church, St Catherine
Site 4.   Zion Sacred Heart Church, Rock Hall
Site 5.   August Town
Site 6.   St Paul's Holy United International Church
Site 7.   Mother Nora's Yard, Westmoreland

Foreword

Edward Seaga

I met Maria A. Robinson-Smith in my constituency, where she worked as a teacher at Tivoli Gardens High School. I was drawn to her because of her interest in and dedication to the areas of sports and culture. I recall the conversations we shared: in a way, I see her as my student who has taken my own research to another level. Her work as a teacher, a cultural activist and later as dance and performing arts coordinator at the Jamaica Cultural Development Commission provided the groundings needed to understand the importance of forms like Kumina and Revivalism to Jamaica's cultural heritage. These forms are critical to studies in memory work, issues of identity and performance practices in Jamaica. It was therefore no surprise to me when she went on to read for the doctorate in cultural studies.

I took note of the way she approached the background studies and fieldwork. Her handling of the Revival iconography in its many modes of symbolism – visual, sound and movement – can be described as ground-breaking. She explored the data collected on seals, symbols, tables, healing rituals and the Watt Town ceremonies in order to advance our foundational understanding of Revival iconography and how it embodies the recovery of self and identity of Revivalists as well as a wide cross-section of African Jamaicans. The photographs included here not only enhance the text but offer additional information to the reader.

This book is crucial in providing information that establishes credibility to Revivalism as an authentic Jamaican folk religion. The following points made by the author must be underscored: the seals, symbols, iconic spaces, rituals and ceremonies, colour codes, dress and accessories are part of a system of knowledge with shared meanings among Revivalists and African Jamaicans across Jamaica and beyond. This system of knowledge also guards and reinvents the African legacy that is very real to Revivalists. The importance of dance to the performance of rituals is emphasized because dance is fundamental to Revivalists experiencing their religion.

This book is an excellent example of how to present the content and context of a traditional folk religion by giving voice to the bearers of the culture. I recommend this book to cultural workers and institutions, the Jamaican populace, the people of the diaspora and the international audience interested in African Jamaican spirituality.

Acknowledgements

Many people in the Revival community contributed to the contents in this book, and to them I am greatly indebted. In this regard, special mention must be made of Bishop Dudley Reid (Daddy Reid), and the leaders and members of the Zion Sacred Heart of Christ Sabbath Church at Holt Close in Kingston. I must also mention Revival leaders, such as Bishop Rudd, Bishop Hill, Mother Nora Dawnes, Bishop Jack and the Watt Town community for the information they shared with me and for allowing me into their sacred space.

The Institute of Graduate Studies at the University of the West Indies also provided me with financial assistance to conduct fieldwork. My research also was supported by a fellowship from the Ford Foundation. Thanks must also be extended to the academic staff of the Mona campus for all the professional support given to me for this research, particularly the late Barry Chevannes and the deputy principal Joe Pereira. I was also fortunate to have the assistance of Clinton Hutton in the area of photography. Outside of the University of the West Indies, I have to thank Diane Austin-Broos and Kariamu Welsh Asante for the valuable suggestions they provided.

I am grateful to my family and friends for the invaluable support they gave me emotionally and financially. In a special way, I say thanks to those who accompanied me to Revival rituals and ceremonies that sometimes lasted all night.

Lastly, my sincere thanks to my mentor and supervisor, the late Rex Nettleford, for all the guidance and support he has given me.

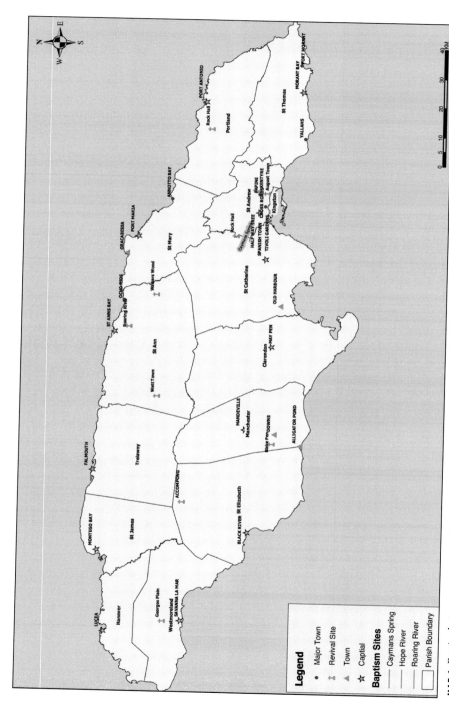

MAP 1. Revival sites in Jamaica. (National Land Agency)

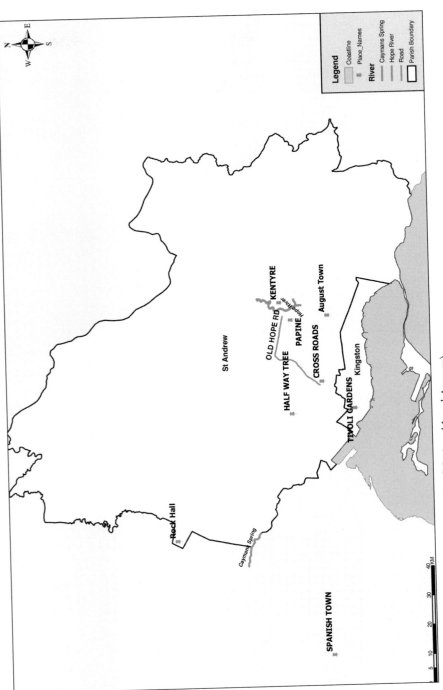

MAP 2. Revival sites in Kingston, Jamaica. (National Land Agency)

CHAPTER 1

Come Journey with Me

Revivalism is an Afro-Jamaican folk religion that was recognized after the Great Revival, which took place in Jamaica between 1860 and 1861. During this time, there were spiritual outpourings of African manifestation, which included African spirit possession in the mission houses all over Jamaica. The result was the establishment of a Jamaican New World religion that was greatly influenced by Myalism and the black Baptist movement. Revivalism not only is a permanent addition to the religious profile of Jamaica but is also deeply rooted and functional in the psyche of Jamaicans of African ancestry.

The Revival cosmology was shaped by the experience of plantation society and sustained by the people's will to survive and transform their new social situation. The notion of a supreme being and lesser spirits in African religion made it possible for the formation of a synthesized cosmology that has at its centre one supreme being, "Maasa God", as well as angels and heavenly spirits, including ancestral spirits and the spirits of departed Revival leaders.[1] The similar notion in Christianity of the Holy Ghost to be received by man made it possible for Christian and African spirituality to co-exist in the same space. Maasa God is also similar to the African cosmological order of a supreme being who is in control of the universe. The Nicene Creed recited in orthodox churches also forms part of the liturgy of Revival churches across Jamaica with one minor change: Revivalists use the term "spiritual church" instead of Catholic Church. The Christian Bible is important to the practice of Revivalism because African experiences can be recalled, reaffirmed and celebrated in the Bible.

The belief that Maasa God is all powerful and controls the universe but is too busy to be involved in day-to-day activities creates the need for relationships to develop between man and spirits. The spirits are closer to human beings and help in the everyday activities. The unity between the supernatural world, the world of nature and the world of man is as central to Revivalism as it is to African cosmological understanding. Everything in nature and the environment can be made active or relevant.

With the centre in place, elements from separate world views that made sense and were reflective of the people's ethos were included in Revivalism and celebrated through the performance of rituals, songs, music and dance, which were integrated into a colourful and rich symbolic system. It is this system that I refer to as the Revival iconography.

Iconography is representation; it refers one to, or reminds one of, something else. By allowing things or patterns to be referred to each other, one is able to interpret them in roughly the same way. Iconography represents important concepts of peoples, places and buildings, all interrelating and creating an awareness of things in form and context. These concepts can inform religious, historical or cultural patterns that are important to the transmission and continuation of cultural forms.

In his historical overview of iconography, Thomas Heck states that, before the nineteenth century, iconography was described as a collection of pictures of important people and portraits of historical personages, but in the twentieth century, it included signs and symbols in art and the sensory codes like sound, movement and smell. "It is more than picturing, it is also about representation and meaning, it includes the sensory code, sound, movement and smell."[2]

The Revival iconography in this context is a collection of the images that relate to Revivalism. There is the presence of Christian icons, such as the cross and the Bible, in Revival churches. Notwithstanding, I choose to focus on those icons that seem to connect more directly to Africa because it is my view that the Revival iconography for the most part symbolically connects to Africa and provides insights into the religious and belief systems of the African Jamaican people. The Revival iconography includes people, landscape, space, dress, objects, symbols, symbolic gestures, music, dance, verbal images, dreams and colour symbolism. The presence of these icons raises the question of the role of iconography in the reconstruction of memory, a system of communication, and how it creates and supports meaning. The

Revival iconography presents a valid cultural medium in the understanding of the folk philosophy of African Jamaican people. This philosophy is so deeply rooted in the psyche of the people that it is often taken for granted and not duly credited.

My Journey

My Revival experience did not begin with formal lectures about the subject but instead began in an informal way growing up in Jamaica. The parish of St Andrew, where I was born, is the home of two famous Revival sites: Hope River and August Town. Hope River has been used as a baptism ground for decades and August Town is the site of Alexander Bedward's church and the famous "healing stream".

During the 1950s and 1960s, as a child living in the area, it was not unusual to be awakened on a Sunday morning around five o'clock by scores of people travelling on Old Hope Road to attend a baptism ceremony by the Hope River. Revivalists from all over the corporate area of Kingston and St Andrew would join the procession along Old Hope Road, and the procession would travel through Papine and down through Kintyre to the point of the Hope River called "Three Hole". Here three big rocks met around a large hole that looked like a pool. According to legend, a "River Mumma" (mermaid) lived in this hole.

During the procession, the people would dance, sing and clap their hands, sometimes to the beat of drums. Most of them would be dressed fully in white with colourful accessories, such as head-dresses, cords and waistbands. The different drum bands were distinguished by their flags and by the styles of their uniform. The flags and accessories added colour to the occasion. The drumming, hand clapping, feet stomping and singing were infectious. People would line the streets not only to watch but also to move to the rhythms and sing along with the bands. Some people followed the bands, joining in with the singing and movement.

In the 1960s, I had the privilege of spending some time with my grandparents in a village called Walker's Wood, in the parish of St Ann. In this setting, I was able to watch and listen to these colourful Revival bands singing and dancing as they made their way through the hills, coming from the adjoining parish of St Mary to hold a street meeting at the Walker's Wood crossroads. As they journeyed along, they carried a "kitchen bitch" (a tin lamp with a wick lit, without a shade) and candles to light their path. At this meeting, they would be joined by Revivalists from the area and other sympathizers or onlookers. They would also solicit new converts for baptism. They organized themselves in a horseshoe or U formation. At the centre of the horseshoe was a table with a Bible and a vase with croton leaves. Near the table were two drummers, an old man and a small boy. The bands would stretch along each side of the table, leaving a clear opening. I later learned that this open end of the horseshoe was not only to provide an entrance for the people going to place their offering on the table but also to facilitate the entrance of the "unseen guest". The uniforms were combinations of red and white, pink and white, and green and yellow.

After the meeting, the members of the local community provided overnight accommodation for the visiting bands. The following day, the bands would continue on their journey to Ocho Rios, some seven miles away, where new converts would be baptized at the historic site at Roaring River. This baptism site is alleged to have been in use since slavery and, like the site in August Town, is said to be rich in healing properties.

FIGURE 1. The procession to the healing stream in August Town, where Alexander Bedward established a healing ministry between 1891 and 1927. (National Library of Jamaica)

I was also privileged to be able to sit and listen to the most fascinating stories about Alexander Bedward from a number of people, one of whom was my grandfather, Earnest Gordon, a Baptist deacon. He had travelled from St Ann to Kingston with scores of other people to be baptized by Bedward. Another person from whom I learned a great deal was Roland Boyd, a Bedwardite. He was one of the surviving "saints" who lived in August Town at the Bedward community. It has always remained with me how deeply moved they were every time they told their stories or recalled events like the healing ceremonies and the march led by Bedward to Half Way Tree Court House with the saints all dressed in white singing "Onward Christian Soldiers, Marching as to War". I knew by the expression on their faces and the fervour with which they spoke, that these events meant much to them and that in recounting and retelling the stories they were affirming their significance.

FIGURE 2. Alexander Bedward between two policemen. (National Library of Jamaica)

FIGURE 3. Bewardites march from August Town to Half Way Tree Police Station. (National Library of Jamaica)

My career path also kept me in touch with Revivalism. As a teacher in a lower-income community in West Kingston, I became aware that many of the students and their parents were Revivalists. The only church inside the Tivoli Gardens community, situated just a few blocks from the school, was a Revival church. Many of the school's ancillary staff who lived in the community worshipped there. It was not unusual for a child to "come under Myal" (be possessed) during school devotion or to be absent from school because he or she was "under Myal". Most of the funerals in the community took place at this church. It was at one of these ceremonies that I first noticed the practice of releasing the spirit of the deceased before burial. The church also played a part in the healing and care of members of the community.

In the late 1970s my studies at the Jamaica School of Dance took me on field trips to two famous Revival centres – Blake's Pen in Manchester, the healing centre, and Watt Town in St Ann, the spiritual mecca of Revivalism in Jamaica. My visit to Watt Town was the beginning of a long and interesting relationship with this site and the people who visit it. From my very first visit to Watt Town in 1978, I was intrigued by the setting and the mystique that surrounded the ceremonies and the people. I never could have imagined a gathering of such magnitude, style, colour and sense of order in the hills of rural Jamaica. The welcome was different from that of other churches. They greeted us with a bunch of croton leaves while singing, "Come in, my little one, come in", as soon as we stepped onto the pavement in front of the church. We were then taken through a welcome ritual. Without any warning or verbal instructions, we just "moved" as we were led counterclockwise around the seal. (The seal is a ritual space and all important rituals are performed on a seal.) This ritual was repeated with all who entered.

The day was packed with excitement, and information was gathered on tape recorders, in notebooks and on cameras by the different groups. When we were leaving, our group was invited to receive gifts. I received a bunch of mint (a herb used to make tea). On leaving the site and entering the bus, we tried to play the tapes that we had made on the site. To our astonishment, they were all blank. I was told later that the reason for this was that we never got permission to record. This reminded me of an observation made by Katherine Dunham, the cultural anthropologist turned choreographer, on her visit to Accompong, a Maroon settlement in the parish of St Elizabeth:

it was important to get permission from the ancestors before any information was shared.

Later, my post as national dance coordinator at the Jamaica Cultural Development Commission allowed me the privilege to observe Revivalism in different parts of the island. As I travelled to and from workshops and seminars, I noticed an abundance of small churches made conspicuous by their names and, very often, groups of colourfully dressed people singing and dancing. The occasion could be a baptism, a funeral or just waiting to go on a "journey".

A most memorable learning experience for me was an assignment to assist with the coordination of the National Revival Ceremony held at Jamaica House in 1986. The then prime minister and minister of culture, the Honourable Edward Seaga, who had undertaken extensive study in Revivalism, organized the occasion. This event, a Revival table held over three days, brought together Revivalists from all across the island. Although the bands had many variations in expressions, colour and performance, they had enough in common to be grouped under the same name and to fit on the same continuum between the poles of Africa and Europe. There were more than two hundred bands from the fourteen parishes. The first night of the table was led by Kapo (Mallica Reynolds) and all the other bands joined in. The second night saw the bands grouping according to the "orders", or categories (for example, Maroon, Bongo). One large group remained with Kapo around the large table with candles, bread, drinks, flowers and other paraphernalia while others went in small groups around ground tables (tables set on the dirt). There was one band that worked around a maypole.

In 1986 I choreographed Louis Marriott's play *Bedward*, which led me to look in detail at the Revival dance vocabulary and to attempt to put this vocabulary in the context of the play. The play was remounted in 2003 and I was again able to bring even greater knowledge to the chorus work through the choreography. In October 2003, I was invited to present a paper at a conference at the University of Cape Coast in Ghana. While there, I was able to visit the town of Kumasi, the Ashanti Palace, Elmina Castle, the Castle of Cape Coast and the Old Koromantse Castle. I also paid a visit to the Koromantse chief and his council. After the offering of libation, they shared with me stories about their history and culture and we discussed possible

Jamaican connections. I was also taken on a tour of the village – both the old section and the new. The Assin Manso Slave Market was another important connection. This was the market from which many ancestors were shipped to the Caribbean. At this site I saw graves with the remains of two enslaved people – Christal from Jamaica and Samuel Carter from the United States. Their remains had been shipped to Ghana in 1998 on the 160th anniversary commemorating Jamaica's emancipation. On the same site was the Slave River where the enslaved Africans were given their last bath before being transported to the New World.

After leaving Cape Coast, I went to Nankopong, the village on which the Jamaican Maroon village of Accompong was patterned. It was in Nankopong that I attended a funeral, visited two spiritual churches and a settlement where the descendants of Jamaican ex-slaves who returned to Ghana lived. The Ghanaian experience allowed me to make some important links between Revivalism and African spirituality. Before going to the field, I spent time looking at the works of a number of authors who did research in Revivalism. The theories put forth by scholars such as Joseph Moore, George Simpson, Edward Seaga, Barry Chevannes, Mervyn Alleyne and Walter Pitts were very important in discussing Revivalism as a religious and social phenomenon. Moore refers to its formation in Jamaica as one of forced contact: "Africans with Africans – Africans which Europeans developed under the process of syncretism borrowing, reinterpretation and invention." Chevannes provides a historical overview that states that the two main sources for Revivalism were "African" spirituality (generally Akan/Myalism-based religion) and Christianity.[3] Pitts stresses the importance of the Native Baptist movement brought to Jamaica by black preachers such as George Lisle from Georgia in the United States.[4] Seaga looked at Revivalism as two sects – Zion and Pokumina – but he also makes reference to twofold bands, a merger of Zion and Pokumina.[5]

Reconstructing an African Identity

This book looks at how Revivalists – through rituals, ceremonies and the setting at Revival sites – use symbolic representation to build and sustain a network of practice and performance while also fostering what Melville

Herskovits refers to as a "grammar of culture" all across Jamaica.[6] Through symbolic productions, they transformed historical data fragmented by slavery and colonization into a system of meaning to create a world that to them is "really real". Clifford Geertz states that "it is this sense of the 'really real' upon which the religious perspective rests and which the symbolic activities of religion as a cultural system are devoted to producing".[7]

The displacement of Africans from Africa to a new location where they were denied the right to belong stirred a need for the creation of institutions that allowed them to respond to the social and cultural issues they were facing. When there is dislocation in territory, origin and culture, people turn to an imaginary homeland to satisfy the need to belong. The rituals and ceremonies are seen as strategic interventions that set the codes and establish the symbols that manifest and express the people's perception of an African Jamaican world view. There is always sharing between the Revivalist and the wider community. This sharing is encouraged and made possible because of the appeal and functional nature of some of its rituals. Because there is no sharp distinction between the spiritual and the secular, people from the wider community can observe and even participate in some of the rituals of healing, "tables" and regular meetings. It is the involvement of the wider society that gives the Revival world view a wide base in the Jamaican society.

These marginalized people were able to reconstruct and fashion an identity in spite of the hegemonic dominance of Europe through the establishment and maintenance of the Revival network. The Revival bands made up of small groups of people in villages across the island and linked by the Watt Town experience are here viewed as a corpus – a pool of information and a collective response.[8]

In looking at the history and culture in Jamaica and across the diaspora, we can see how African patterns and vehicles of knowledge reside in the memory of the descendants of Africans. Therefore, in order to understand Revivalism, it is necessary to familiarize oneself with the channels of expressions and cultural patterns in African history. Emphasis is placed on selected symbols as channels of communication, their use, the meanings they generate, the actions and movements they inspire, and their philosophical underpinnings. Important to this discussion is the notion that "culture is philosophy as lived and celebrated in a society".[9]

The Revival church is an archive of African Jamaican memory, preserved through the various seals and symbols that make up the Revival landscape. These symbols are represented through the visual, sound, smell and movements. Inscriptions on the walls, the ground and the body are credited as forms of writing. In this study the Revival space is therefore explored as a space where memory of the distant past, the immediate past and the present intermingle. The Revival seal was explored as a liminal space that enables the participants to access ancestral wisdom through communication with spirits. It is one such space "betwixt and between" where crossovers are negotiated between the human and spirit world.[10] The ceremonies, rituals and bodily practices were studied in order to understand "how memories are constructed, conserved and repeated".[11] The symbolic representations, which include signs, music, dance, rituals, colour and dream symbolism, are examined for the meanings they create, the values and philosophy they endorse, and the role that the iconography plays in formalizing and structuring the rituals and ceremonies. Also important to this work is the deployment of the iconography during the performance of rituals and ceremonies.

Dance and the body in motion are important to this text because it is through the body that Revivalists experience their world and it is through the body that the link between the human and spirit world is facilitated. The link to the spirit world, the world of their ancestors, is key to the meaning and function of Revivalism.

My Approach

In this book, I drew from the experiences gained at the different stages of my life on which Revivalism has had an impact, because these experiences forged a conviction of the importance and validity of this work. I used the information gained from what has been written about the subject to configure a theoretical framework. Using history, oral history and the belief systems of African Jamaicans, I have attempted to establish a genealogy and definition of Revivalism. Looking at the genealogy or groundings of Revivalism is important because it is my view that the iconography is the result of an ancestral heritage passed down through many generations of African

Jamaicans. The oral history and the stories told to me by grandparents and others helped to provide insights into the world views and culture of the Revivalists.

I have used the actor-centred approach, which gives credence to what people say, what they do, and why these acts are important to how they understand and experience their religion. This approach allows for the creation of new texts and a vision of African Jamaican epistemology. Repeatedly attending performances of the same ritual (for example, healing ceremony) at the same place among the same people and going to the same rituals at different churches conducted by different people allowed for a greater understanding of the ritual process. This approach also allowed me to focus on individuals in specific performances, especially the leaders, who understand the rituals and lead the performances.

Participation in ritual processions and ceremonies allowed me to use my body as a research tool to experience, document and store information, especially in dance and movement. This also gave me a chance to bond with the practitioners themselves: two of the members of a Revival church gave me access to their personal archives in the form of pictures, audiotapes, videotapes and programmes of church activities. The symbols and settings were also documented through photographs and videotapes.

It is important to note that our folk culture has survived over the past four centuries through oral and non-verbal communication traditions preserved through storytelling, songs, music and dance, and rituals. The Revival community, like most of the Jamaican society, is non-scribal. Even today when people are functionally literate, they tend to write only when it is really necessary or when they cannot do otherwise. Profiles of key Revivalists were useful in providing information on people's life histories, their world views and their day-to-day activities. These were profiles of individuals involved with the leadership and organization of the church at Holt Close. Interviews were conducted at the church at Holt Close as well as at their offices, homes and on the sites of the different ceremonies. People from the other churches and the sites visited were also interviewed. The brand of Revivalism known as 60 is also called original Zion and displays more Christian elements while the brand of 61 displays more Africans elements: the views of both the informants who were associated with 60 and those who are associated with 61 are included because the religion was studied along a continuum and not as different sects.

There was much to be gained by listening to the people who came to watch the ceremonies or just to sing along. Many of them, although not devotees, understood the process and made useful comments, especially concerning the naming of events, happenings and sequencing. Overhearing such comments, I was sometimes able to ask direct questions and get clarifications on the naming of certain rituals and icons. It was also important to listen to and look for the different cues in the ceremonies, because they indicated what icons were brought into play.

Descriptions of the fieldwork are given in order to frame the ritual practices in a manner as close as possible to the people's performance of these practices. Only after this do I attempt to analyse or interpret the material presented in order to further the understanding of this unique Jamaican cultural form. Key to understanding this cultural form is underscoring the importance of inheritance from ancestors and the cosmology in the contemporary Revival community.

The Zion Sacred Heart of Christ Sabbath Church, along with its environs, was studied as a sociocultural location for African-derived forms in Revivalism. A full description of the church setting is given, placing the icons and symbols as they appear in the physical structure. The processes in the church that kept the African Jamaican memory alive and allowed for African patterns to be preserved and recreated through its rituals and ceremonies are presented. In order to understand the people, I observed the organizational structure, symbolic objects, privileged spaces, artefacts, cosmograms and dress that impacted the ceremonies either directly or indirectly. The profiles and programmes are relevant because it is the people who have the knowledge of the iconography and give spiritual efficacy to the religion.

Through photographs, some of the seals and symbols that form a part of the Revival iconography have been identified. These include colour symbolism because colour in Revivalism functions as an icon. As Stuart Hall has said, "Signs stand for and represent our concepts, ideas and feelings in such a way as to enable others to read, decode or interpret their meaning in roughly the same way that we do."[12]

Attention has been paid to the structure of the rituals and how the iconography articulates the Revival cosmology. I focused on the healing ceremony/ritual because it is the most popular in all the churches and has an enormous outreach to the wider society. The elements of the rituals and ceremonies are treated as cultural performances that facilitate the retrieval of ancestral memory and institutionalize the belief systems of Revivalists. Hence, music, dance and movement dramas are treated as icons that allow for human transformation. The importance of performance to the success and survival of the rituals and ceremonies is hereby underscored.

An overview of the more public iconic space at Watt Town is presented through its history, its mission, its physical setting, the people who use the shrine, their dress and accessories, and the spaces of power. The seals and symbols are compared with those of the other churches visited both in form and concept. The Revivalists' yearly pilgrimage to Watt Town was studied in an effort to understand what this journey meant to the people and how the icons were used to give clarity and meaning to the rituals. Having followed the activities of the bands on one of their trips from their home church to Watt Town, I call this journey an ontological journey, and it was organized in seven suites.

Through symbolic representation, African connections were made and identity markers for African Jamaican people were thus established.

CHAPTER 2

Grounding in Revivalism

In order to understand the formation and development of Revivalism, the historical, social and cultural records of the Jamaican/Caribbean people must be taken into account. It is also important to look at the Caribbean space as an arena where those with power negatively affect those without power. The meeting of different peoples from different cultures was bound to create friction, especially in circumstances of involuntary exile. This friction was made worse by differences in ideology and belief systems of the conquerors and the conquered.

For over five hundred years, Europeans imposed their own paradigms on the people they conquered. Through slavery and colonization, they forced African peoples to see the world through European eyes – "the eyes of the other". The enslaved were alienated from their traditions and were made to feel that their culture was inferior unless it was refined and schooled in European ways. According to Robert Young, "The inferior races at home and abroad had to be civilized and acculturated into the ideological dynamics of the nation."[1]

The hegemonic paradigms most successfully used to demoralize people of African descent were race, religion and culture in all its other aspects. Institutions such as the Christian church and the formal political establishments justified these paradigms. Christianity and the classical heritage of Europe were the two most effective vanguards. They designed and fostered modes of living that were deemed proper, moral and civilized by European standards while race established the guidelines for the relationships in plantation Jamaica.

All across the diaspora, African people created their own paradigms to counter the hegemonic paradigms of the oppressors. In some instances, they adapted and syncretized existing forms and expressions in order to make them relevant to their needs. Some of these paradigms were resistance, Maroonage, transformation, accommodation, adaptation and, in more recent times, constructs such as Negritude, Africanity and Black Power.

All of these theories and practices have formed part of the counter-resistance used by a people forced to survive within a culture oppressive to their existence. Cultural forms described as resistance in motion and as being counter to modernity have sprung up across the African diaspora. The Shouters of black America, Santeria of Cuba, Shango of Trinidad, the Spiritual Baptists of St Lucia and Barbados, Candomble in Brazil, Vodou in Haiti and Revivalism in Jamaica are all manifestations of cultural resistance. In referring to the Jamaican world view, Chevannes asserts, "I call this worldview Revivalism from the religion of the same name and argue that the driving force in its formation was the people's determination to make the best of this new situation on their own terms."[2]

Before and after emancipation, this religious network came under serious attack from the plantocracy as well as from the established Christian churches. The authorities banned possession, dancing, drumming and herbal practices, deeming them subversive, but this did not stop the practices. For example, the drum rhythm was preserved and practised through sound and body movements. Our Caribbean scholars Edward Kamau Brathwaite, Rex Nettleford and Barry Chevannes have written extensively on the importance of these forms to resistance.[3] In Chevannes's view, maintaining one's image is a form of resistance, a political response that functioned as a liberating force. Through their religious rituals and ceremonies, Revivalists temporarily gain release from everyday pressures and are empowered and energized to cope with their personal problems. In response to the question, "What has kept all these people in Revivalism over the years?" Bishop Reid, the highly respected Revival leader, replied, "It is hope, when everything around them has failed; it gives you courage to go on."[4] This confirms the point made by Herskovits that religious belief was at the core of slave resistance. The presence of the priest assured leaders of supernatural support. These beliefs gave them the conviction that the powers of their ancestors were aiding them in their struggle for freedom.

Resistance as a creative response was manifested through the development of new cultural forms in Jamaica and the Caribbean. These forms served as a continuation of African patterns as well as in the creation and posturing of an identity of difference, as a means of remembering, as a form of cultural inscription and as a language.

In a lecture on Caribbean creative diversity, Nettleford, speaking about the redemption, renewal and rebirth of a culture, supported his argument with the following quote from Derek Walcott: "The tribe in bondage learned to fortify itself by cunning assimilation of the religion of the Old World. What seemed a surrendering was redemption. What seemed the loss of tradition was its renewal. What seemed the death of faith was its rebirth."[5]

Redemption, renewal and rebirth were made possible through bonding. The peasantry and slave quarters brought a unity and togetherness among the African enslaved groups that inspired and produced forms representative of African ritual practices or belief systems – dance, song, chant and the making of instruments to produce the sounds to which they were accustomed. African Jamaicans practised these values in the slave quarters, free villages and in the fields in order to remake and refashion their culture. They created common bonds by whatever means they had, but the strongest of these bonds was through religion, hence a religious network became entrenched in the island. These religious practices persisted in spite of the banning of certain religious forms. In 1842, after the ban was lifted from Myal practices, Hope Waddell, a minister of religion, described a Myal Revival meeting in Western Jamaica as "the strangest combination of Christianity and heathenism ever seen".[6] He could not understand what was taking place. It was also notable at this Revival meeting that most of the participants were members of the Baptist Missionary Society.

The Genesis of African Jamaican Spirituality

The two groups most often referred to as displaying or reflecting a Jamaican style of worship were Myal practitioners and the Native Baptists. Research based on a number of secondary sources presents the possibility for establishing some kind of genealogical connection between the Myal religion and the Koromanti people. Myal was the established religion of the Maroons, who regarded themselves as Ashanti and Koromanti. The name Koromanti has been traced to the Fanti settlements in the Gold Coast, where the English had established early trading posts for the slave trade in 1631. The village of Koromanti, which still exists, was a barracoon, or holding post, from which enslaved Africans were shipped to the Caribbean.

The early Maroons were runaway slaves who lived in the mountainous interior of the island. Most of the early Maroons came from West Africa and were brought to Jamaica by the Spaniards. After the English took control of the island in 1655, the number of runaway slaves from plantations increased. These were enslaved Africans who challenged the oppressive system and took steps to free themselves from the shackles of slavery. This act of running away was an act of resistance to slavery in more ways than one. First, it was an attempt to escape by withdrawing their labour from their enslavers. Second, it allowed for the establishment of communities of Africans who would not only be the organizers of serious rebellion but also the preservers of African culture. According to Joseph Williams, "Myalism then was in reality the old tribal religion of Ashanti with some modification due to conditions and circumstances. It substantially featured the veneration of the minor deities who were subordinate to Accompong and included communication with ancestral spirits."[7]

Among the Maroons and among other groups across the island, the enslaved Africans who stood out – whether in number, dominance or both – were the Koromanti (also known as the Coromantee). Due to the influx of Akan slaves, from 1655 until the abolition of the slave trade in 1807, the enslaved were shipped from Cormantee and Elmina, the Gold Coast of West Africa. These people belonged to two main language groups – Akan and Ga-andagme – and shared the same cultural traits. Jamaican slave owners preferred the Akan, as it was argued that they were tough and hardworking.

British slave traders on the Gold Coast also sent a flood of war captives to the West Indies from the Ashanti kingdom:

> He was an old Coromantee, who with others of the profession had been a chief in counseling and instigating the credulous herd, these priests administered a powder, which being rubbed on their bodies was to make them invulnerable. They persuaded them into a belief that Tacky, their generalissimo in the woods, could not possibly be hurt by the white men, for he caught all the bullets fired at him in his hand and hurled them back with the destruction of his foes.[8]

It was the Ashanti religious practices that brought Coromantees and other Africans together all across the island.

During the early half of the period from 1655 to 1700, the largest single group of enslaved Africans came from the Akan and Ga-andagme peoples of the coastal strip of Ghana. The number of slaves from Ghana was greatly reduced during the eighteenth century and the majority at the time came from other areas like Nigeria, but there was always a steady flow of slaves from the Akan-speaking people. In *The Sociology of Slavery*, Orlando Patterson states: "Almost every one of the serious rebellions during the seventeenth and eighteenth centuries was instigated and carried out mainly by Akan slaves who came from a highly developed militaristic regime, skilled in jungle warfare."[9]

Records of the many Akan revolts speak eloquently to the Akans' resistance to bondage. The strengthening and bonding of these escapees were also facilitated by a number of events surrounding the harsh brutality meted out to the enslaved on plantations. These events united not only the Maroons but slaves and blacks in general.

Before looking at this connection, it must be made clear that there much strife between Maroons and the wider slave population. There was also much rivalry even among Maroons who shared a common Coromantee background. This was so because the different ethnic groups among them still maintained the distinction of their origins; for example, there are three distinct burial plots in the old cemetery at Accompong: Coramantee, Asante and Kongo. These enslaved Africans came from different countries, spoke different languages and were not able to communicate effectively. Hence there was tension and mistrust among the different groups. In addition to the ethnic or tribal differences among Maroons, the divide-and-rule tactics of the British increased this tension. This divide was formalized by the peace treaty with the Maroons in 1739 in which Maroons pledged to assist the government in the suppression of all future rebellions.

In spite of all these difficulties, the Maroons and other members of the black population still managed to join together against the tyranny of the Europeans. The ability of the Maroons to unite the different tribes rested on their use of a special agreement, referred to by English anthropologist Robert Sutherland Rattray as the Asante Legal Maxim, which prevented a tribe member from disclosing the origin of another individual.[10] It was the creole blacks, however, who played an important role in bonding the Maroon and enslaved communities, because by the end of the eighteenth century they had outnumbered the African-born slaves, and more so because they were all born into the same sociocultural environment:

> It was these Creole Maroons, with no competing or cross-cutting loyalties, who helped to anchor the new ethnic identity of the Maroons; they provided a solid and unquestionable core to which it attached. Whether their ancestors were Coromantees or Madagascars or Spanish Maroons, their common experience could outweigh the differences in their land of origin far more easily than it could for the Africans who had lived in those lands. For Creole Maroons, those far lands were mythical. Furthermore, since Maroons born in the same societies had grown up together, there was little strain of adjustment. While they might have spoken the various African and European languages of their parents at home, and practised some of their traditions in private, they also learned from childhood, the Creole English and the common culture of their Maroon society. It was their primary reference group and they had no serious competitors for their loyalties.[11]

Chief Cudjoe, the head of the Windward Maroons, was said to be the brother of Nanny, who was the head of the Leeward Maroons. The military genius of Cudjoe and the cunning and powerful bush tactics of Nanny were key characteristics of the Maroons. Cudjoe, working with his brothers Accompong and Johnny, who were his chief assistants, does have some resemblance to the organizational framework of the Ashanti/Akan family lineage and military style.

The Ashanti tradition of naming their children by the days of the week also seems to have been followed. Joseph Williams, who has written extensively on Ashanti retentions among the Maroons and in Jamaica, cites examples of Ashanti names (such as Cudjoe, Quaco, Cuffe) as well as the retention of proverbs and folk heroes. He writes, "NyanKopong became the Accompong of Jamaica just as Obeah-man was a transition from Obayifo."[12]

There were many rifts and even treaties that worked against the unity of Maroons and the enslaved population. A counter to this divisiveness was the mythical genealogy of two sisters, Fanti Rose and Shanti Rose, who chose separate paths.[13] Fanti Rose chose the path to freedom by whatever means

– bush, battle, Myal dance – while Shanti Rose, mother of the enslaved, chose the path of least resistance. Kenneth Bilby suggests that this was a symbolic means of mending the split and extending the kinship ties to all blacks, because whether they were the children of Fanti or Shanti, they were one black family.

The emotional unity and sentimental bond that held plantation black communities together was possible through their experience on the slave ships, Koromanti dominance, the extended family and the coming together through inter-African syncretism within a broader framework of Ashanti. This coming together of different tribes was familiar to the enslaved in Jamaica, as the pattern of uniting under the banner of one ethnic group was generally true across the Caribbean and Plantation America – Yoruba in Cuba, the Fon people (Dahomae) in Haiti, Bantu in parts of Latin America, Yoruba in Brazil, Akan in Suriname and Jamaica. "Whether in estate village or in the greater privacy of their own settlement, Africans had to face the fact that they could not reproduce exactly the societal order of their home communities. So they built something new out of the old principles, recreating the experiences of Africans enslaved in Jamaica."[14]

The shared religious rituals and ceremonies practised among Maroons and other Africans created the synthesis necessary for unification. The Jamaican Maroons' recognition of Yankipong (Nyame) as the supreme being as well as ancestral spirits followed the practice of West African Akan worship, with the supreme being at the head of the pantheon and lesser spirits called Obosom. The practice of sacrificing goats, which is associated with the veneration of Asasi, the earth goddess, and the belief that ancestral spirits link the world of spirits with the world of the living are also traits that are distinctly West African. The Akan/Maroon worshipping practices also include the priest (Akamfo), dance, and communication between deities and human beings. This pattern of worship was one to which other nations of Africa could relate.

A. Opoku states that the only visible sign of worship for Nyame was an object called the "Anyansedua", which translates to "tree as God".[15] A pot was put on the forked branch of the Anyansedua to collect rainwater (referred to as God's water) to sprinkle the members of the household. As John Mbiti writes: "Akan chiefs keep on their compound a three-fork branch of a tree, used as an altar. This is known as God's tree."[16] Akan religion was established among the Maroons in the form of Myalism, and in the wider society it became rooted in Revivalism.

The Myal man or priest was an important figure in Myalism. He was the intermediary between the people and the spirits. Myal men were leaders both physically and spiritually. Their role was to protect individuals from personal as well as social problems. Hope Waddell once observed a Myal ritual dance and described it as follows:

> There we found them in full force and employment forming a ring around which were a multitude of onlookers. Inside the circle some females performed a mystic dance, sailing round and round and wheeling in the centre with outspread arms and wild looks and gestures. Others hummed or whistled a low monotonous tune to which the performers kept time, as did the people around, also by hands and feet and the swaying of their bodies. A man who seemed to direct the performance, stood at one side with folded arms quietly watching the evolution.[17]

The essence of Myalism is spirit possession. The syncretism that took place between Akan religion and Christianity was not only responsible for the survival of Myalism but also provided an abundance of leaders who came mainly from the Native Baptist movement. Myalism, though inclusive of other African practices, was less inclusive of Christianity and, as a result, it remained for a long time the storehouse of African religious practices and way of life.

Myalism first came to the attention of the Europeans during Tacky's Rebellion in 1760 – the most serious slave rebellion to that point. It was led by Tacky, a Coromantee chief from Africa who was enslaved on an estate in St Mary. Before starting the revolt, all Coromantee and Akan slaves swore a sacred oath administered by the Obeah-man in the same way that the Ashanti priest in West Africa performed ceremonies that made Ashanti warriors invincible to the attacks of the enemy.

The strength of Tacky's Rebellion was that it was fought not by tribal links but along Myal/pan-African lines and it included all African ethnic groups. The strength of the Akan leadership was that it did not prevent inclusion of the other ethnic groups. Myalism and most other forms of African religion had the ability to absorb and transform other religions; thus, the distinction between Myalism, Native Baptist and Christianity was often blurred.

Black Leadership

The Native Baptist movement was probably the group that was most responsible for spreading Myalism in Jamaican society. The movements that came after 1776 were sometimes referred to as the more Christianized version of Myal and were associated with the black Baptist preachers from the United States. The black Baptist leaders were revered for their dynamic leadership. George Lisle came to Jamaica from Georgia during the American Revolutionary War and established a church at Race Course in Kingston in 1782 named the Ethiopian Baptist Church of Jamaica. During the same period, Moses Baker, who was described as George Lisle's lieutenant, started a congregation in Cook Spring, St James. Two other African American preachers who settled in different parts of the island were George Gibbs and George Lewis. Gibbs's mission was mainly in the parish of St Mary while Lewis worked in the parishes of Manchester and St Elizabeth. They laid the foundation for Sam Sharpe, Paul Bogle and Alexander Bedward to follow.

There were different black religious groups, both during slavery and after slavery: there were mission groups affiliated with the established church and the estates as well as non-affiliated native religious groups. In all of these groups, the leaders were outstanding members of their communities. The white missionaries would set up a class in a house in the areas where church members lived and appoint a black member of the community as leader of the class. The success of these leaders, especially the Baptists, was due to the fact that they usually chose someone who was already acknowledged by the people as a chief among them. He was therefore chosen not necessarily because he was a good Christian but because of his leadership skills. This charismatic leadership style was preferred, as these leaders could attract a large following. The fact that they were black also gave them legitimacy to lead and communicate with the people much better than the whites could.

The 1831–32 Christmas Rebellion (known also as the Baptist War and the Black Family War) led by Sam Sharpe (Daddy Sharpe), a leader in the Native Baptist movement and a deacon in the Baptist Church, was organized through the church class leadership system and is recorded as the most successful rebellion in Jamaica.

Oaths were used in this rebellion. The enslaved were sworn to secrecy by taking the oath in a manner similar to that used in Tacky's Rebellion. Leadership was centred on Sharpe and the leadership of the black Baptists who were predominantly creole. In both the Tacky and the Sharpe rebellions, the leader did not have a problem combining religion and politics. This was possible because religion and politics were inseparable in African cosmology and, by all accounts, the same can be said of the Jamaican cosmology.

In 1831 the majority of the enslaved on the island were creole-born. The rebellion was organized by Sam Sharpe at a time when the socio-economic and political situation on the island was particularly stressful. The enslaved had become increasingly dissatisfied with the system of oppression. They were also conscious of the pressures being placed by the Anti-Slavery Society on local authorities and on the British government for improved conditions for enslaved people. The enslaved blacks were also aware of the resistance to any kind of improvement to their conditions and especially to abolition. The enslaved used the machinery of the church to organize the rebellion. They quoted the scriptures to justify the cause. Bible verses such as "no man can serve two masters", "God created all men equal" and "the freedom of the children of Israel from bondage" were linked to the struggle for freedom in Jamaica. Sharpe and other black preachers did not use the teachings of the Bible to preach about life in the next world but instead to speak to the oppressive conditions of the present world.

Myalism and the Native Baptist movement were the preferred religions of the enslaved and ex-slaves. These religions were popular among the people because they were relevant to the people's struggles. The black leadership that emerged was concerned not only with saving souls but they were united in the struggle for better social and economic conditions for the masses.

The church was the cohesive base that unified and galvanized the efforts of the Morant Bay Rebellion of 1865. Paul Bogle and George William Gordon, who led the rebellion, were considered by the people as spiritual and political leaders. Bogle, a Baptist deacon, was associated with black solidarity and led petitions for greater access to property. The Native Baptist Church provided the forum for Bogle and Gordon to articulate the problems of the masses. The reports cited in the British *Parliamentary Papers* of 1886 gave many examples of how the black population used colour, religious rituals, and symbols such as the Bible and the flag as unifying agents of the rebellion.

The following are excerpts from the British *Parliamentary Papers*, which show examples of practices and rituals relating to the existence of an African Jamaican spiritual complex as expressed in the 1865 uprising in Morant Bay: "A mob dancing and blowing horns and the flying of a red flag as an emblem of their new-found solidarity and strength of purpose."[18]

The Bible was used to take the oath of allegiance to one's colour. "The people shouted, 'colour for colour', 'kill him'. The man shouted, 'I am Manning of the Maroons' and a tall man ran up and said, 'peace, peace, save him'."[19] It was also reported that Bogle told the people not to kill a man who identified himself as a Maroon. From the reports, it is clear that colour and religion were unifying agents of the rebellion. In another example, the parliamentary commissioner asked J. Harrison, a witness, "Had there been anything to attract your attention previous to this outbreak?" and Harrison replied, "Yes, a great deal. . . . I have been on the property ten years. For the first six years the people behaved very well; after the revival, there was a great difference."[20] Harrison noted that the Revival "about four years ago was among the lowest class of Negroes". The commissioner then asked Harrison what he meant by "revival". Harrison answered: "I can hardly tell you, but they all stopped working and began to pray and jump about."

Eleanor Shortridge's statement on 29 January 1866 gave an account of the people carrying flags on bamboo poles just before the burning of the Morant Bay courthouse. This could be a reference to the carrying of flags in Revival religion. One could assume that the people were summoning the spirit forces to war. G.S. Osbourne, in his testimony on 27 January, referred to the fact that the "people were compelled to kiss the Bible and to take an oath. . . . 'You kiss this book that you join your colour, so help you God.'"[21] The flying of red flags, the oath of allegiance to one's colour, jumping, shouting and dancing were the elements used to bond the black people together under the themes of religion and politics.

Bedwardism was another strong branch of the Afro-Christian religion. Alexander Bedward, a charismatic preacher and one of the first elders of the Jamaica Native Free Baptist Church, was a contemporary of Marcus

Garvey. Bedward led a thriving ministry in August Town between 1891 and 1921. The forerunner to the religious institution that Bedward headed was H.E. Shakespeare Wood, a black preacher from the United States who started the church in 1888.

Bedwardism focused on the struggles of the black masses; its message was anti-colonial and spoke to the racism and the political aspirations of the people. He saw black people rising up to take control, and he believed that the black wall would rise up and crush the white wall. Bedward, described as the first Revival shepherd and the father of Revivalism, is recognized as a great leader and prophet. In 1891 he declared that in one of his visions the spirit had revealed to him that "water from the Hope River, a stream flowing in August Town, could be turned into medicine for body and soul", and he was convinced that through water baptism, the oppression placed on black people by white people could be removed.[22] His preaching attracted thousands of followers from across the island who regarded him as a prophet from God come to deliver them.

Marcus Garvey, born in 1887, echoed the sentiments of Bedward for deliverance of the oppressed and redemption for the black man: "Up you mighty race; you can accomplish what you will."[23] Garvey's mission was to liberate Africa from colonialism. He continued the protest pioneered before him by Tacky, Sharpe, Bogle, Gordon and Bedward. Garvey, like most of his predecessors, saw the church as a liberating force, hence his mission was supported by a strong black theology. Chevannes compared Garvey and Bedward to two great biblical characters: "Bedward and Garvey [were] was as Aaron and Moses, one the high priest, the other prophet, both leading the children of Israel out of exile."[24]

The Revival cosmology embraced both religion and politics. The shepherds, deacons and leaders used their knowledge of African religion and the fact that they were black and understood the struggles of black people to hold together a religious network across the island.

The Revival Continuum and World View

The Revival continuum runs between the European and the African poles. The African end of the pole is strongly influenced by Myalism, Kumina,

Convince and other African-derived forms. Kumina and Convince are blood-bond groups, which link them to particular African nations. Kumina is linked to the Kikongo and Convince to the Bongo nation, in the same way the Maroons are linked to the Ashanti. African religion was able to take root in Jamaica for a number of reasons. People take their religion with them wherever they go, and the Africans who came to Jamaica were no exception. Many brought their belief systems and memories of their gods, and as there was hardly any substitute religion in the first 150 years of their coming to Jamaica, their religions survived. The Roman Catholic Church of the Spaniards and the Anglican Church of the English plantocracy made little attempt to meaningfully incorporate the enslaved population. Most of the other religious groups – fundamentalists and Protestants – started missionary work on the island beginning at the end of the eighteenth century. By that time, African religions had taken root, made easier by the fact that African religions are not confined to church on Sundays but are a part of the everyday existence of the individual.

The other end of the continuum – the European – is orthodox Christianity. Although the Anglicans, Methodists and Baptists were probably more established, the Moravians were the first to arrive on the island in 1754.

The Anglicans provided a working creed that allowed for reinterpretation according to individual understanding. This creed was the meeting point on the continuum between African and European religions. It was taught to the enslaved in the mission schools, and they then recited the creed on Sundays. The principles of the creed did not conflict with the African concept of religion. God the Father Almighty, maker of heaven and earth, the supreme being, was for Africans the creator of all things. The Holy Ghost/Holy Spirit, which is manifest through man, had its parallel as well in the African world where spirits manifest themselves through human beings; the African unity of the spiritual and physical world was therefore made central to the African Jamaican world view. The creed is still repeated in Revival churches with one notable substitution: the Holy Spiritual Church is used instead of the Holy Catholic Church.

Rivers and streams are important to African mythology and religion; therefore, water baptism in Revivalism provides another important point of contact. It was this set of shared beliefs that laid the foundation for the merger of the African and Christian traditions. Revivalism was born out of the integration of different religious systems. It must be remembered, when analysing or looking at the Revival continuum, that there are varying shades of interpretation, and the way different groups integrate will depend on their interpretation and cultural lineage.

At the middle of the continuum there are several variations that reflect the people's history, religion and belief system but across groups: "Although Pokumina, Revival and Baptist are normally different they are points on a continuum of differentiation; Pokumina is the closest descendant of Myalism, Revival or Revival Zion and various forms of Baptist show greater degrees of Christian influence."[25]

African gods or spirits are more active and recognized in some forms of these religious movements and less so in other forms. Edward Seaga claims that there are some bands that practise both Zion and Pokumina.[26] In this interchange, "whether whites borrow from blacks or blacks from whites nothing has remained pure: neither pure African nor pure Christian".[27] So, in spite of the variations on the Revival continuum, it provides a space described by Noel Leo Erskine as a comfort zone in which black people could be black. "Revivalism offered a context in which the membership was able to express themselves in their own way and it provided a setting in which black people can accept themselves, affirming that they are accepted by their God."[28]

This continuum can be looked at from different perspectives: historically, socially, politically, as well as aesthetically. The historical perspective is important because different historical factors affect the continuum. In the case of the Caribbean, different peoples came to the region at different times; hence, different influences either became dominant or added to the mix. The different influences facilitated the shifts and repositioning of ideas for emphasis and focus – hence the changes on the continuum. The continuum from European religion to African religion provides a large space for different groups to worship according to their own taste and belief, although not without tension. Nettleford refers to such tension as the "battle for space".[29] However, in my opinion, Revivalism is more about the sharing of a space.

In order to have the better of two worlds, there has been masking and dualism – masking in the sense of Christian symbols being used as a cover for African worship. It is always interesting to look at what is taking place during Revival Bible readings and the singing of hymns. These run concurrently with other ritual practices. Some Revivalists are also members of the Anglican, Methodist, Baptist or other orthodox churches and do not have a problem with maintaining ties with both religions.

There is no sharp distinction between the spiritual and the secular, hence people from the wider community can observe and even participate in some of the rituals and regular meetings. This sharing is encouraged and made possible because of the appeal and functional nature of some Revival rituals. It is the involvement of the wider society that gives the Revival world view a wide base in Jamaica. The fact that Revivalism is found in every parish – both in urban and rural areas – reinforces Chevannes's claim that "Revivalism is indeed national in scope and character".[30] The world view is a work in progress that is kept relevant through revision and the transformative process. It is a creative process that remains alive through the dynamic interplay of symbols.

Revivalism, like its forerunner Myalism, is focused on keeping alive the links with the ancestral spirits through rituals and ceremony. Revivalism created a space where African Jamaicans could practise their religion to fulfil their spiritual needs. It offered its followers healing and protection from harm and provided individual and community security, as well as a feeling of well-being. All of these were important to a people dispossessed and broken by the harsh realities of slavery and poverty. Revivalism has its strongest and most loyal support among people from the poorest class of society and, by extension, those who are also predominantly black.

The Importance of Symbols to the Study of Revivalism

Symbols are critical to the meaning and purpose of Revivalism. The ways in which symbols are used by the different groups suggest strongly that there is enough common ground for them to be classified as one religion. Many scholars have put forward some views on the importance of symbols to the religion.

Two significant symbols are "the seal" and water. The seal is the centre for the most important ritual activity within the Revival church. Water baptism is significant as a rebirth of the individual not only in a Christian sense but also as a reconnection with Africa. In traditional West African religions, for example, the Dahomey River cults use immersion to create a "new born brother". This custom has existed in Jamaica for a long time. Robert Stewart states:

> In March of 1842 there appeared in the *Evangelical Magazine* a letter, signed by "Vindex", on Baptist churches in Jamaica. The writer observed how the one who was being baptized would be greeted affectionately by friends as he came up out of the water with the words, "Oh my new-born brother, I am glad you got through so well." Vindex continued: "No one is ever so addressed till he is baptized, and generally the particular phrase, which is a household term, occurs at the precise period of baptism. The propensity of Jamaican blacks for baptism can also be connected with the Asante belief in the divine origin of water, the belief that every river or important body of water was related to the Supreme God as a son of God. Bodies of water were looked upon in Asante as containing the power of the spirit of the Creator; as a woman gives birth to a child, it was believed, so is water to a god or son of god."[31]

The use of water by Revivalists aligned more with the African context than with the Christian missionaries' context. The total immersion in water was not only sacred to African Jamaicans but was a source of healing. Other symbols in Revivalism include the croton plant (a representation of African spirituality), the candle, the flag, the Bible, the coconut and Kananga Water. In the following chapters, I examine how symbols facilitate the reconstruction of memory and create and maintain a system of iconography that sustains the Revival outlook. These will be discussed where they bring meaning to the rituals and ceremonies being observed. I look too at the relevance of colour and codes in interpreting Revivalism, as well as at how music and dance facilitate rituals and ceremonies in Revivalism.

CHAPTER 3

The Revival Church

On this rock I will build my Church
and the gates of hell shall not prevail
against Zion
—Inscription on the church wall at Zion Sacred Heart

The Zion Sacred Heart of Christ Sabbath Church is located in one of Kingston's inner-city communities. The programmes and activities that sustain the group and allow them to practise their religion are many and varied. The processes in the church keep the African Jamaican memory alive and allow for African patterns to be recreated through the rituals and ceremonies. The people, organizational structure, symbolic objects, privileged spaces, artefacts, cosmograms, dress and colour have an impact directly or indirectly on the ceremonies. It is through these practices and the belief systems of the practitioners that the symbols are imbued with meaning and one is able to understand the Revival space.

"Member meaning", as explained by members of the community, is important in the descriptions and naming of events. It is also important to get close to the true meanings as generated by the people's experience, not only by what they say but also through their gestures, body language and how they interact with each other.

The Church's Hierarchy and Organization

The people at Sacred Heart are hospitable and friendly. They are keen on talking to each other between and after sessions and receiving counsel from the Father Bishop. Young men and women in the community who are not converts are made to feel comfortable in the setting. They share in the rituals and ceremonies and even share jokes with the elders. Although most of the members come from the lower socio-economic group, there are some professionals in the membership. Among the ranks are teachers, nurses, civil servants and entrepreneurs. There is also support from the middle class, artists and businesspeople, who do not attend the church but sponsor tables and pay fees, which they feel are necessary for the ephemeral renewal of continued health and financial success. The church is part of the Revival network across the island. This network is maintained by keeping in contact with Revival communities in most of the parishes. A high point in their activities is the journey at least once a year to Watt Town, the mecca of Revivalism in Jamaica.

The church is perceived by its leader and members as Zion or 60 (which refers to the original Zion), but the leader and hierarchical members do still recognize the presence of "61" in their midst. One man in his testimony said, "wherever there is 60 there is 61". Seaga describes 61 as Pokumina.[1] One member refers to 60 as "sky order" and 61 as "earth order". Bishops Reid and Bourne speak to the presence of 61 among many of the members. Neither of them see it as a problem as long as the leader is in control. From my observation, the bands are more inclined towards 60 than 61, but they could be described as following both groups, as Seaga points out.[2] In the practice of Revivalism, 60 is close to the European end of the continuum while 61 is closer to the African end.

The church hierarchy and positions held by core members are described as the "Board of Governors" in the programme for their 2002 convention. The names of the rest of the people who attend church do not appear on the list; even those who have hosted duty tables are not listed. Some of the functionaries listed in earlier printed materials are not mentioned on this particular list, but the leaders and members function in much the same way as those with the old titles like bands messengers, bands warriors, armour bearers, dove, hunters and others. The following short profiles on a few of the senior leaders and members of the church provide some background on the key people, their world views and their roles in the church.

Archbishop/Daddy Bishop Dudley Reid

Bishop Dudley Reid is the head of the diocese of the Zion Sacred Heart of Christ Sabbath group of churches. He is the leader and founding father of this church, which celebrated forty-one years in 2002. The bishop, like all other recognized folk heroes or leaders, has a sense of mystique to his existence. Born in Troja, St Catherine, where he received his first call to service from the "messenger" at age thirteen "to go to Lime Hall in St Ann to do the work", he worked in the church in Lime Hall until the spirit sent him to Rock Hall at age seventeen. At Rock Hall he studied with Father Bogle, a spiritual man who was the leader of a band in that area. Reid describes Bogle as "deep in Maroon" – that is, well-schooled – and reports indicate that people came from all over the island to learn from him.[3] The unusual and elaborate design of Bogle's final resting place speaks volumes. It is a shrine where people still visit to offer food and gifts to the deceased. Bishop Rupert Bourne described the church at Rock Hall as "one with a lot of spiritual work, healing and not a lot of preaching". Reid describes Bogle as his spiritual leader who taught him spirit work; he refers to his sojourn at Rock Hall as "a journey on which spiritual things were explained to him".

FIGURE 4. Site 4, the shrine built to house the tomb of Father Bogle – the tomb is shaped like the star of David (2004)

FIGURE 5. Site 4, Father Bogle's tomb is kept furnished with food, drink and other gifts from the people in the community (2004)

Reid sees the journey as pivotal to his spiritual development, as he believes that a leader must understand the different religious "orders" or ceremonies to be able to deal with them. He prides himself on his being a leader who has mastered the Maroon, Bongo, Come-See and Church message orders, and one who can control all of these orders. He calls himself a Maroon and states that "Maroon can work with all the orders". He goes on to cite some of the orders: Maroon, Fire, Water and Ministry Work. He says that water is very important to the message of this church and that "water is a definite order and must be on the seal especially for the Saturday message when you use water right through. Fire is not always used in the church and when you work with fire, water is not used." Fire, he states, is used for cleansing and moving things: "Sometimes you have seven fire holes, left according to how you set the order."

Bishop Reid is a performer – he knows how to hold a group together and to satisfy his flock. He knows how to distance himself from his participants in order to hold his audience in awe. His entry for a healing or table ceremony is quite dramatic. After the preliminaries have been carried out by the bands, he makes his entrance and the church stands in respect. He holds his body erect and he makes no eye contact with anyone; he goes directly to the table where he inspects the setting and then lights a candle before moving to his chair. From his position on the platform, he looks at his bands and the setting. When he is satisfied, he waves to the church; the church responds by waving their hands and saying howdy-do. He is a charismatic leader and an excellent dancer. His dance competence is a reflection of how he feels about

FIGURE 6. Site 1, Bishop Dudley Reid at Watt Town, circa 2008. (Clinton Hutton)

dance. As he once said, "Dance is powerful; it is deliverance; it is life." Bishop Reid suffered a stroke in June 2001 and has lost most of the mobility on his right side. When he was invited to the opening of the Sacred Heart Church in Canada, he declined. The members of the church tried to persuade him, but he would not change his mind. I decided to visit with him at his home to find out why he would not even discuss the subject of going to Canada. I felt that although he had lost most of the mobility in his right leg, he was well enough to travel. After a long discussion, in a tearful tone he said, "If I go, I will not be able to dance and if I cannot dance, it makes no sense."

Bishop Rupert Bourne

Bishop Rupert Bourne is a telephone technician and a resident of Canada. He started in the faith when he was fourteen years old. He grew up in Kingston with his grandmother, who was a Revivalist and a descendant of the Maroons. At age sixteen, he started to grow spiritually under the guidance of Bishop Reid. He learned different movements and the different sounds of the drum in order to communicate with the spirit force. "You learn certain secret orders in spirit work," he once said.

Bourne understands spirit work and believes that one cannot be a bishop if one is not grounded in spirit work, but it is his wish "to open the church to more modern ways of doing things in order to carry the church through". His robing ceremony was an example of a more modern practice. In the old way, done by Reid, "he would have been wrapped in a white sheet and rolled all over the church". He took that ritual out of his ordination and kept it more like that of any orthodox church, except for the blessing of the ceremonial clothes. During the blessing there was dancing and "blowing of notes" by Bishop Reid and a group of senior bishops and pastors of the Revival hierarchy in Jamaica. Each garment was danced around by different members of the group before he was robed. This session was the most spiritual part of the ceremony and lasted for about an hour out of a four-hour ceremony. Prior to the robing ceremony, there was a coronation ritual that took place one Sabbath at the church. During this ceremony, the bishop and pastor were stripped of all jewellery and their shoes and anointed. This took the

FIGURE 7. Bishop Bourne and the bands, dressed in khaki and gold, working the seals at Watt Town

form of a complex ritual dance drama done without any announcements to the members of the church or any other group of people. One pastor said it was not planned, but was directed by the "messengers". This ritual was also done to facilitate Bourne leading the band through the rituals at Watt Town on the yearly pilgrimage. On the first Thursday in March 2002, Bishop Bourne journeyed with the church bands to Watt Town for the first time as their leader. As he led the bands around the seal, two senior bishops guided him through the process.

Bishop Bourne sees the church as serving Jamaicans internationally. He is the founder of a number of churches in Canada, the United States and England. He is articulate, sings well, is a good dancer and a charismatic leader.

The Overseer Pastor/Journeyman – Christopher Morrison

The overseer pastor Morrison is in his early forties and works as a driver and sometimes as a security guard. He can quote the Bible on almost any subject and he is described as deeply spiritual by Bishop Reid. His grandfather was a Revival shepherd and his grandmother a Maroon from St James. Morrison did not know his grandfather but he met him in a dream. In the dream, his grandfather reportedly said to him, "Come mek a give you a bath." It is with this experience and others that he credits his beginnings in Revivalism. He has spent much time with Bishop Reid and regards him as his spiritual father.

As superintendent, he visits other churches and sees that things are in order. In his spiritual work, he journeys in order to receive messages for the church. "He works deep, working through 60 and 61, getting utterances from the spirits for the group. He works with water, he is a water man." When he is in the spirit, it is like the performance of a dance drama. Although he travels deeper in the spirit than any other member, including the bishop (Reid once said of Morrison, "Him travel deep, not even me don't go so far"), Morrison was not chosen as bishop-elect. There are those who feel that it is his inability to control how far he goes in the spirit world that rendered him an unsuitable choice for the number-one leader. It is felt that the leader must be in control.

Church/Flag Mother – Mother Beverly Davis

Mother Beverly Davis is described by both Bishops Reid and Bourne as "deeply spiritual", and as one who knows the orders: "She knows what she is doing; she can clear the bands using the flag." When she dances with the flag, people classify the patterns she makes curling the flag in the air and around objects as a work of art. She is precise about the orders and follows the correct procedures in doing things. She is also not afraid to challenge any of the leaders if she thinks things are not going right. This has earned her a reputation of being cantankerous or "maddy-maddy". She is described by Bourne and Pastor Queenie Brown as Miriam, the guardian angel of the church. She takes an active part in all the rituals.

Pastor Queenie Brown

Pastor Queenie Brown is what Jamaicans would describe as a high-brown lady (or mulatto). People of her colour are not usually seen in Revival churches. Her grandmother had a seal in Point Street, St James, near Kensington, and her father played drums. This has been her religion all her life. She was "put down" by the spirits for twenty-one days (meaning, she embarked on a twenty-one-day journey). She got up with a "big blue and gold four pole table, four corners of the earth, four power angel of the Earth".

Queenie believes that she was chastised by the spirits for being too proud to do the work and that putting her down for twenty-one days was a way of humbling her. She is a good leader and a beautiful dancer. She moves her arms like a swan, her back is supple, and she relevés like a European classical ballerina. When she is in the spirit, the carriage of her arms and back gives the impression of someone trained in the Graham (modern dance) technique. When she "cuts away" in the spirit, she stands on the bench and dances like a bird perched on a tree limb. Her son is the bell ringer, a duty he has assumed since the illness of the senior bishop.

Mother Yvonne Richards

Mother Yvonne Richards lives and works in the rural hills of St Andrew, about two miles from Golden Spring. She was born in the parish of St Catherine

FIGURE 8. Altar in Mother Yvonne Richards's yard (2004)

but grew up in the parish of St Mary with her mother, who is a Revivalist. She describes her mother as one who has the gift of healing and has an "office" in her yard. She also remembers her great-grandmother and her grandfather as healers: "They all did healing and reading at home." The family line of Revivalists runs from great-grandmother to grandfather to mother to daughter. This makes Mother Richards at least a fourth-generation healer.

Mother Richards lays claim to the fact that she works with Bongo spirits: "It is a family tradition as one of my daughters can work it, she can knock the bongo drums." She boasts of having done spirit work since she was eight years old. "I could tell my mother that the bands are coming and they would come. I used to warn at school." She was born in 1954 and she has been giving baths for more than thirty years. She specializes in giving baths instead of medicine because the people believe in baths. "They believe in it more than medicine," she says. She gives different kinds of baths, such as spiritual, prosperity, sickness and warm baths. The setting in her office has all the major symbols of the church – flag, water, healing jar, Bible, croton and a rod. She has a special species of croton which she calls the "jevic". This is important to her work: "It is like Psalms 70 to me." (Psalms 70 refers to God as deliverer and protector and calls on believers to magnify Him.) The dance is also important to her work, especially for clearance and deliverance: "Dance is for deliverance – David danced for deliverance to recover the covenant of God. The spirit puts you in a dance and it is used to release people from sickness." Mother Richards runs a thriving business as she is also a "reader". She is the cornerstone of the church at Sacred Heart (by that, I mean one of the biggest sponsors), and they rely heavily on her for financial support.

Lesma York – The Chief Organizer

Lesma York has been a member of the church since 2002. She was previously affiliated with the Church of Christ fraternity, as her husband is a minister in that church. She was invited to Sacred Heart by Bishop Bourne and maintained a visiting relationship for about two years before accepting the right hand of fellowship. She is a "water messenger" and the chief organizer. Her duties are, as the title suggests, to assist with organizing the different activities in the church. The main function of the chief organizer is to monitor the uniforms or dress code for the different ceremonies.

The General Membership and other Roles in the Church

The members of the church find employment in different fields. A few are professionals, teachers and nurses. Other popular vocations are clerical workers, secretaries, security guards, ancillary workers and domestic helpers. One interesting vocation is that of the missionary. The missionary table mother (Sister Vicki Carmen Ricketts) runs the "drop pan" and lotto shop in the nearby community. "Drop pan" and lotto are games people play to win money and are both associated with gambling. I find this interesting because it speaks to a cosmology that has thin lines between the sacred and the profane. In most orthodox Christian churches this would not be openly tolerated, but Sister Vicki is able to do this job and still remain close to the bishop. She is "his favorite song bird who brings in the messenger". Gambling is not in conflict with the principles of this church.

The missionary or table mother, who plays an important role in setting the orders for the different ceremonies, is the daughter of the owner of one of Kingston's oldest drug stores. She is knowledgeable in the choice of colours for different occasions and the oils and paraphernalia necessary for the success of different rituals. The church's secretary is a teacher in one of the country's traditional high schools, and the assistant secretary is a supervisor in one of the halls of residence at the University of the West Indies.

The vineyard mother assists with the physical arrangement of the church. She makes sure that all the objects needed for the rituals are in place, that the church is kept clean and that the plants are cared for.

The members of the bands are divided into about three groups:

1. In the first group are members who understand spirit work. They are described as deeply spiritual people who understand the rituals and can initiate, lead or facilitate the spiritual journey. An example of these would be the church mother and others who understand the workings of the spirit.
2. Another group of members are those who are Bible people, who know the scriptures well and can go from verse to verse to illustrate their points.
3. Then there are the organizers – those who see to the physical needs of the church and arrange and plan for the many functions on the church calendar.

There is evidence of some overlapping of groups, but the very senior members of the church are usually versed in all three areas; for example, the church mother, water mother, armour bearer, pastors, elders, mothers and water messengers all understand their role and the workings of the spirit.

Programme of Activities

Members of Zion Sacred Heart of Christ Sabbath Church participate in a wide range of activities throughout the year. The church meets on Saturdays for Sabbath school in the mornings and vesper service in the afternoon. The first session of Sabbath school, which starts at ten o'clock, is mainly Bible study and singing of hymns. The vesper service is more spiritual, with much singing, dancing and exhortation. Monday evenings are reserved for healing service. The Women's League meets once a month in the church on a Sunday to conduct its business meetings. The other Sundays of each month are used to visit other Revival churches or to engage in activities at their home church. These activities include Bible study, prayer meetings, motivational talks and recreational activities.

Other activities include the Women's Day Convention in April, the Bishops' Three-day Thanksgiving Table in May, Candlelight Service in June, the annual seven-day convention in September during which the memorial table for a priest is held, and also the ritual blessing of the handkerchief, and a concert in December. Baptisms, christenings and duty tables take place throughout the year as the need arises.

The level of interaction and sharing among Revival groups is very high. The church in Kingston is the head of the other Sacred Heart churches and keeps in touch with the group mainly through visits to the thanksgiving table, duty tables and special functions like baptisms and robing ceremonies. The church also plans small group visits to other Revival churches in St James, Westmoreland, St Ann, Trelawny, St Catherine, as well as all over the corporate area of Kingston and St Andrew to attend ceremonies and rituals. An exciting ceremony is the early Sunday morning baptism at Caymanas Springs. This locale has become more popular over time than Hope River. On any given Sunday morning between six and eleven o'clock, the atmosphere at Caymanas is like a water carnival. Also popular is the yearly journey to Watt Town, one of the oldest functioning Revival sites in Jamaica. This takes place every first Thursday in March.

Other areas of interaction among Revival groups are the visits, reading and healing sessions that take place in the more private spaces of the homes of individual members. Different people have different gifts – healing, reading, cutting and clearing – and all these gifts are shared, sometimes for a fee. These special services facilitate a number of people who share the Revival world view but do not wish to associate publicly with the form.

The church has a diocese with local and overseas branches. The local churches are in the parishes of Kingston and St Andrew (urban and rural), Clarendon, St Ann, and Trelawny. There is a branch in New York, United States, and one in Toronto, Canada, and links are being set up in London,

England. The church, through the work of the bishop, also has connections in Costa Rica. This is the pattern throughout most of the strong Revival churches. They have links in the countries to which Jamaicans have migrated over the years.

The Setting of the Church

The church is positioned east to west with the altar facing the east. It is divided into four sections. The first area is the platform where the church hierarchy sits on one side with the pulpit on the other side. At the back is an altar beautifully adorned with flowers, candles and different ornaments. Above the altar, the writing on the wall reads: "On this rock do I build my church and the gates of hell shall not prevail against Zion." On the wall there are pictures of a deceased bishop and one of an elder. To the right of the altar is a mirror. On the wall next to the mirror is a door that leads to the bishop's reading room and the exterior.

The second area is the front of the altar where there is a rail that separates this section of the church from the other. Hanging from this rail are many flags and banners of different colours. Leading from the altar is an area that is probably the largest part of the church. In this space is the church seal on which a large table is placed. This table is central to most of the rituals that take place in the church. There are always water and croton leaves on this table. The colours and arrangements on this table change depending on the nature of the function, whether it is a thanksgiving or healing ceremony. To the left of the table, just in front of the platform, are two Revival drums. These are most commonly used when a ceremony requires a drum, but during some celebrations a drum set is added to the same area. To the right of the table, just in front of the altar and adjacent to the walls, are two small tables – one with a pail of consecrated water, a mug and some glasses, which are used during the healing ceremony. The other table carries a large earthen jar of water to which a special attendant is assigned to stir or "till" the water. The jar is described as a "healing seal". A similar jar was seen at the home of a Revivalist healer and reader just in front of the healing room in her backyard. Going down the line on the right side of the church, parallel to the wall, are a chair and a bench. On the left side are two chairs. Then there are two doors – one on the right and the other on the left. These provide a straight passage across the church, linking the church to the outside. Along the walls in this area are hanging flags and writings. Similar signs and drawings can also be seen at other Revival sites and bear a close resemblance to the *veve* in Haitian Vodou. Beside the left door is a stairway leading to the balcony. This middle section of the church is very spacious. It is the largest open space of the church and allows room for people to dance during the different ceremonies.

The third area of the church is centred on the pews where the congregation sits. There is an aisle that runs down the centre of the church, separating the pews into left and right sections, and the aisle is wide enough to accommodate plenty of movement. On the wall is a picture of the late bishop of the church, a young man, the son of the senior bishop, who was murdered in front of the church. (The senior bishop had groomed his son to take over his ministry but he [the son] was murdered a few years after he was robed.) Band members and visiting friends sit in this area during the ceremonies.

The fourth area, which is immediately in front of the church, and the surrounding environs are also interesting. This area is like an enclosed front patio with its boundaries being the front wall of the church and the front fence of the church property. This area was described by the bishop as the "entertaining area" because it is sometimes used for events that would not be accommodated in the church, such as Kumina drumming. To the left side of this area is a small shop, and a driveway is to the right. The space between the front wall of the church and the fence is loaded with symbolic paintings, artefacts and two pools. One of the small pools is painted white on the outside and blue on the inside. Depending on the occasion, the décor of this pool could include candles of different colours, vases with flowers or green plants, bowls or cups with different mixtures or some other paraphernalia deemed necessary for the ceremony in progress. The other pool is called the mermaid pool.

There are a number of symbols in this area, the most imposing being the sculpture of a mermaid (called a river mumma) situated to the right of the entrance door. Just beneath the mermaid is a rectangular pool with water, seven stones and three turtles. "The river mumma brings power to the church", says Bishop Reid. The river mumma is also described by Bishop

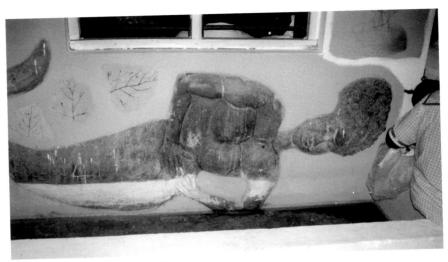

FIGURE 9. Site 1, mermaid pool (2001)

Reid as very powerful. These symbols seem to depict what is most important to the different orders of the group. As the bishop puts it, "the mermaid is a very high order, as a matter of fact it can work many orders".

To the left of the entrance door is a vase with flowers, two keys, a chain, a sculpture of four white candles and one black, a jar and an interesting sculpture of a man's bust with two swords crossed above the head. There is also a painting of a snake and a pot with fire.

The symbols drawn on the left side of the door include a snake, candles, machete, fire and a chain. These resemble some of the symbols that represent the *loas* in Haitian Vodou. Harold Courlander states that in Haitian Vodou, Dambala is represented by a snake or the rainbow.[4] Ogun is represented by the chains or iron bar, Shango/Michael by the machete, the colour red, and the pot of fire.

Also in front of the church and close to the fence are two tree stumps surrounded by stones. In the circle around the tree stumps there are growing plants. Courlander describes the setting: "In the court, the bases of four sacred trees are surrounded by circles of masonry low brick walls."[5] Although Courlander mentions four tree stumps, there are only three at Sacred Heart.

To the left of the church is a small shop where refreshments and other items are sold. Behind the shop is a garden area with a pool with fish. The

FIGURE 10. Site 1, sculpture of a man's bust with two swords crossed above the head (2001)

pool was described by a member as a symbol of life in water. Behind this area is the four-point seal. (The importance of seals to spirit work will be discussed later.)

At the back of the church are some private spaces. To the left there are two reading rooms. One is the bishop's reading room, in which there is a life-size sculpture of a mermaid, a bath, the bishop's desk and other artefacts. The other reading room is used by one of the senior mothers of the church. Also at the back of the church are a few rooms that help to ease the burden of some members in the church who have housing problems, and there are additional rooms that are used as temporary shelters for visiting bands or for pilgrims on spiritual journeys.

The people, the setting and the symbols are all important to the production of meaning and the formation of concepts among Revivalists. It is in celebrating the rituals and ceremonies that the people give meaning to these signs and symbols. The signs store the knowledge necessary for the people to interpret and experience their religion. In his book *Representation*, Hall states: "Signs stand for and represent our concepts, ideas and feelings in such a way as to enable others to read, decode or interpret their meaning in roughly the same way that we do."[6] The members of Sacred Heart and other Revivalists are indeed able to read and interpret the meanings of the signs and symbols in the church in roughly the same way. These signs are also representative of the values of many generations of African Jamaican people.

CHAPTER 4

Seals and Symbols That Form Part of the Revival Iconography

Seal crown all
Bible to Book
Seal crown the work
—Bishop Dudley Reid

The Revival iconography is necessary to the practice of the religion because the meanings generated by these icons make them integral to all the ceremonies and rituals. Whether it is the setting of a table, a healing ritual, a baptism or an ordinary service, the use of seals and symbols plays an important role in members' function and the production of meaning of the particular ceremony. Seals and symbols make up the repertoire of images (iconography) that represent the collective eye of the Revival culture. The colour of the candle, the flag and other symbols all help to develop a system of shared meanings. Barbaro Martínez-Ruiz speaks to the importance of objects as spiritual vessels that store the knowledge necessary to experience religious practices: "It is through these signs, symbols, seals and objects that participants are able to understand and communicate with each other."[1]

Robert Farris Thompson refers to graphic writing systems as powerful spirit forces, with cosmograms acting as codes to attract such forces.[2] Paul Connerton refers to signs as a people's struggle against forced "forgetting" and highlights the importance of these signs to social memory.[3] The writings on the seals are forms of communication with the spirit forces. Revival practitioners and devotees all across Jamaica understand these codes because they are a cluster of sacred symbols woven into an ordered whole that ultimately make up a religious system.[4]

Every race and hybrid possesses cultural components that are different from any other and that reflect their own unique world view. The Jamaican Revivalists certainly fit that description, as their traditions offer a glimpse into Jamaican social history, aesthetics and world view. Icons serve as a means of differentiation and as statements of power and quality. Church members sometimes boast among themselves as to whose icons are better and more powerful miracle workers. The Revival tradition is mainly an oral tradition with information residing in memory, and this information forms a pool of knowledge or corpus. There are structures within that corpus that facilitate the flow, exchange and validity of this information.

Revivalists document and exchange information in two main ways: inscriptions, which are drawings and writings on church walls, and seals and performance or body practices, for example dance, music and rituals. Revivalists make a distinction between seals and symbols, and I have organized a collection of photographs accordingly. There are times also when a symbol and seal are used interchangeably.

Definition and Importance of Seals

The epigraph of this chapter, from Bishop Dudley Reid, states without a doubt the importance of the seal to the practices in Revivalism. The seal functions as a liminal space for the enactment of ritual performances. Seals are found not only in churches but in homes, yards and some public spaces. These privileged spaces are central to the activities that take place in Revivalism. At the Zion Sacred Heart of Christ Sabbath Church there are seven seals on the site, according to Bishop Reid; each carries out different orders and functions, and each can convey different messages. Reid says, "The seal signifies the different letters; then you say the order is so or so." These spaces (seals) are best understood in relation to how events are structured and played out in these areas. Different communicative actions take place in these spaces, hence the practices can be defined or interpreted according to the space in which they occur. Different functions can also take place in the same space at different times; for example, the messenger seal can become the space for the healing ritual on a Monday or a Wednesday. At Watt Town, the welcome seal or office becomes the revelation seal between noon and three in the afternoon. Bishop Bourne, who has established a Revival church in Canada, explains, "Different messengers bring in different messages or revelation at different times."

Bishop Reid's statement that "Seal crown all, Bible to Book, Seal crown the work" can be interpreted as meaning: in the same way you read a book to gain knowledge, you work the seals to acquire knowledge. The many seals and the working of different orders suggest that each seal represents a different body of knowledge in the same way books cover different subject matters.

Leader Edgar Linton of the Watt Town church noted that "the seal is a place from which blessings are received". He also refers to one particular seal as "Sunday School", where one learns about the principles of the religion, and another as an "office", where the Revivalists "sign in", registering their presence on the grounds to do spirit work. Linton also refers to the seals as deliverance grounds.

Bishop Bourne, working on the physician seal, describes the spot as a place where people come for spiritual upliftment and to share the experience: "On this spot, if we are worthy, certain angels can hand to us that which we must take back to our congregation; certain angels can hand to us on this spot that spiritual upliftment." While taking a younger bishop through the drills on the seal, Bourne made the point that it is important that those who have the knowledge share it with others. He went on to chant: "Me come fe share all that we have. From Genesis to Revelation me come fe share all that me have." Bishop Edgar Hill describes the seals as very important to the church: he says, "We get a lot of revelation here." Bishop Rudd makes the point that the "seals are used for different functions and represent all nations of Africa and India too".

Bishop Reid noted that there are different ways of working the seals. This, he said, depends on the letters of the alphabet and orders used. "Not everybody can work the seals. You have to know how to set the orders for different things and how to read the messages." Reference is also made to the opening and closing of seals: "Seal is like a vault with a code; if you don't have the code you can't open it." Bourne said he watched Bishops Reid and Humphrey Reid in order to learn "what notes to follow and what keys they used". Based on my observation, Revivalists work the seals by making sounds and by moving in an anticlockwise circle around the seals. The sounds can include the blowing of notes, drawing sounds, cymballing and movements such as trumping or marching.

The conception and creation of a seal is a spiritual experience. All of the Revival leaders I have interviewed about their special seal told me that the seals came to them in either a dream or a revelation witnessed or displayed by other beings. These beings in the Revival world could be ancestors, spirits of departed Revival leaders, prophets or angels. Dreams are a means of communicating with the supernatural world and provide a source of knowledge on religion, cosmology, history and culture. This contact with the unknown allows Revivalists to access knowledge that would have been otherwise inaccessible. The dream symbols are treated by Revivalists as truths and symbolic messages to be displayed.

Classification of Seals

The seals are permanent objects or defined spaces that can be described as culture specific. They represent the core values and systems of belief in Afro-Jamaican culture. All the major rituals of the church are performed on a seal. The healing ceremonies, tables, rituals of anointing and ritual dramas take place on or around particular seals. These are ways of preserving and transmitting knowledge other than through writing in books. They also give clues or links to ethnicity, providing information about the religion, healing, spiritual upliftment, deliverance and the sharing of knowledge. These seals represent what Geertz described as inherited conceptions passed down from one generation to the next.[5]

The seals in Revivalism could be classified in the same way that African shrines are classified. Dominique Zahan classifies the seals into four basic elements: air, earth, water and fire.[6] In Revivalism they are represented through the four-point seals and four-point tables set for thanksgiving ceremonies:

- Water, in the African context, is seen as a source of life. Water shrines include rivers, lakes, springs, vases with holy water and, in a few cases, sea temples. In all the Revival churches, water seals are represented in the form of pools, water jars and basins. They are associated with water spirits, particularly the river mumma. There are also many springs and river holes that hold special significance for Revivalists.

- Air "consists of sacred trees and groves that act as an intermediary between human beings and sacred powers".[7] Many Revival sites have trees that function as seals; these sacred trees are sometimes circled with stones and surrounded by plants, or the trunk is covered with a cloth of many colours. Groves of croton flourish in Revival yards, especially at Watt Town. To the Jamaican Revivalist, the croton is representative of African spirituality.

- Earth shrines have been described as having many variations, including mountains, rocks, caves and stones. "The earth has no edifice; it is a religious and sacred monument in itself", states Zahan.[8] The earth and ground seals in Revival yards and the church, which are kept in contact with the earth, fit in this group. The messenger seals in most Revival churches are in contact with the earth. Ground tables set for African night or special duty tables are sometimes set on the earth.

- Fire is described as the mediatory element between the living and the dead. Every time I have seen fire used at a Revival ceremony, it has had to do with dispelling an evil spirit, or seeking intercession for cleansing of a space, or seeking permission to use a particular space. Most Revivalists use fire when it is thought necessary. Mother Nora is the only one I have met who keeps the fire seal burning all the time.

For Revivalists, the seals function as a crossroads between the human and the spirit world and also as an instrument of social unification. The seals provide the main areas for the performance of spirit work, hence they facilitate the bridging of the gap between the human and the spirit world. During the performance of spirit work, the seals function as a stage on which the divine and human worlds connect. On this stage, the living offer libation and sacrifice to the spirits in return for gifts of healing, ancestral wisdom and spiritual communion.

Most of the sites visited have seven seals. There were some leaders who felt that to disclose information on the seals in their church was to lose their power or let loose their secrets. Based on the fact that the leaders of six churches, plus Watt Town and three Revival yards, allowed me to visit their seals and from what I heard and observed while attending rituals and ceremonies at other churches, it is safe to say that if not all Revival churches have seven seals, then most of them do. The names of these seals are similar in some instances but different in others.

The seals found on all the sites visited were the four-point seal, messenger seal, water seal, physician seal and entertainment seal. These seals varied in appearance and sometimes names at the different sites but they all were named by their bands according to their function.

Some Common Seals in Revival Churches

Four-Point Seal

The four-point seal, located under the shed at Sacred Heart Church in Kingston, is regarded as the highest and most powerful seal on the compound. "It is the highest seal and different revelation can be drawn there. Not everybody can work it, as it carries many different orders," Bishop Reid noted. It is sometimes called the deliverance seal or the Myal or Maroon seal. On the wall near to this seal is a reference to Jerusalem school room, the twelve tribes of Israel and the order of Melchizedek and the prophets. Bishop Hill

FIGURE 11. Site 1, four-point seal at Sacred Heart Church, Holt Close, Kingston (2002)

from Gethsemane United Church makes reference to the four-point seal as the pilot seal, a leading seal and the central seal. A four-point seal was seen on all Revival sites visited. On some sites they are more elaborate than others, but on all the sites they symbolize the four elements – water, wind, earth and fire – and the notion of receiving messages from the four corners of the earth.

FIGURE 12. Site 3, four-point seal at Gethsemane United Church, St Catherine (2004)

FIGURE 13. Site 4, four-point seal at St Michael's Church, August Town (2004)

The Messenger Seal

In all the churches visited, the messenger seal is located in front of the altar and near the centre of the church. It is on this seal that the table or a centre pole is positioned. This space is used for the rituals of everyday service, healing service, duty tables, thanksgiving tables and the baptism ritual (the vow). This is where most tables and rituals that involve the whole church are held. The table is usually decorated or set to suit the ceremony being held. The messenger seal in all the churches visited was unique.

Water Seals

Bishop Reid refers to the pool in front of his church as a high seal. It brings in all kinds of orders. "Sometimes devotees go in and travel through different cities," Reid said. Mother Nora Dawes from Georges Plain, Westmoreland, hints at the connection of pools to "the river Euphrates and the river Nile running all the way, the city carry everything". Both Reid and Dawes stress the importance of water seals to the religion and the connection to Africa.

The healing jar is another water/healing symbol. This jar is always tended by the vineyard mother or one of the members who work the water order. At different points during the healing service, the attendants stir the water. At all the sites the mermaid/river mumma and water spirits are important to the spirit work of the bands. During possession, the people connected to water spirits perform dance dramas based on the spiritual encounters they have with the water spirit.

FIGURE 14. Site 1, pool in front of the church at Holt Close (2002)

Welcome/Entertainment Seals

There are two welcome/entertainment seals at the front of the Sacred Heart Church. The visiting bands enter from this area, but these seals are also used for welcoming and entertaining the spirits during the "come-see" ceremony, which is held on the night before a memorial table or after a three-night table is held. On one of these seals is a dove-stand with a candle that is always lit and on the other a pole with four prongs. In the centre of the four-pronged pole there is a basin of water, and there are bottles of water on each prong. There are flowers planted around the seal. Bishop Bourne made the point that this is the area where all the spirits come, but not every spirit is entertained in the church. The stranger seal at the Gethsemane United Church is used in the same way as the entertainment seal at Sacred Heart.

The physician seal is located near the healing jar and sometimes near the areas designed for baths. These seals are found in many Revival churches, including Watt Town. There is a physician seal in the bishop's reading room at Sacred Heart. At Watt Town, there is one near the little rooms used for baths.

Special Seals

All the churches I visited had at least one special seal: a seal representative of the leader's spiritual calling, whether as a healer, a reader or a journey man.

The special seals at three different churches were as follows: Site 1 (Holt Close) had a merman sculpture and a bath, Site 2 (St Michael's) had an Indian hut and a pool, and Site 3 (Gethsemane) had the hunter seal, dove seal, and the bongo-man seal. The hunter is the bishop's seal because he is a hunting shepherd. The dove is the seal of the senior mother, while the bongo-man seal is that of the senior male pastor. At Site 6 (St. Paul's), the special seal is called a tree house seal and at Site 7 (Mother Nora's) it is referred to as the all-nation seal.

The merman seal is located in the message room, otherwise called the spiritual office, of Bishop Reid. The seals in the message rooms of the different churches take various forms depending on the leaders' spiritual guide. At Sacred Heart, it is a sculpture of a merman positioned at the far corner of a bath.

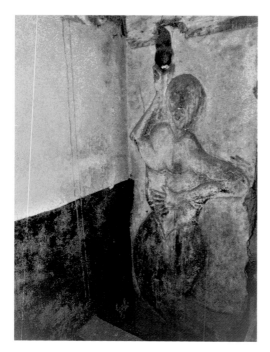

FIGURE 15. Site 1, merman sculpture positioned beside a bath in the message room at Zion Sacred Heart of Christ Sabbath Church (2004). (Clinton Hutton)

FIGURE 16. Site 2, the leader's special seal – a combination of a pool and an Indian house surrounded by crotons (St Michael's) (2004)

FIGURE 17. Site 3, the hunter seal with machete (Gethsemane) (2003)

FIGURE 18. Site 3, bongo-man seal (Gethsemane) (2003)

Although Sites 1 and 2 did not have a bongo-man seal, the leaders under-stood and could work the bongo order. Sites 1 and 2 also did not have a hunter seal, but the hunter was represented in dance at the different ceremonies at all the sites. Only one of the leaders mentioned had a permanent representa-tion of the Indian presence in Revival. Many of them prepare a temporary structure during their thanksgiving tables. The Indian presence is also strong in the dance practices.

Some of these seals can be found in nearly all Revival churches. The presence of certain seals depends on where the particular church is on the continuum and whether it is what most Revivalists call original Zion 60 or 61 – one- or twofold. All the seals function as a bridge between the human and the spirit world.

Tree House Seal

The tree house seal could be described as an African house because of the items stored inside. The seals at St Paul Holy United International Church (figures 19, 20 and 21) were created by Leader Wollery. Leader Wollery was

FIGURE 19. Site 6, St Paul Holy United International Church (2004). (Clinton Hutton)

FIGURE 20. Site 6, seal and alter in the tree house seal. (Clinton Hutton)

FIGURE 21. Site 6, altar inside the St Paul Holy Internation Church tree house seal, with sev tiers (2005). (Clinton Hutton)

respected for his work in the African order. He was responsible for training many Revival leaders in the African order.

Mother Nora Dawnes's Seals

Mother Nora was intro-
duced to a large gathering at
Georges Plain, Westmoreland,
on 30 December 2005, as the
African Queen of Revival.
Mother Nora is committed
to Revivalism. Like Mother
Millie (Millicent Vassell) and
Leader Wollery, Mother Nora
had the opportunity to reside
overseas but chose to remain
in Jamaica. All three believe
that if they do not do the work
they were called to do they will
suffer from illness or bad luck.
There are some seals that give
Mother Nora's yard its African
characteristics: they are the

FIGURE 22. Site 7, all-nation seal in Mother Nora's yard, her special seal (2005). (Clinton Hutton)

African hut, the all-nation seal, the all-nation hut, the all-nation pole and the fire seal. Mother Nora added a pool for the first time in 2005 because she wanted to stay on the "African way". She went on to say, "I added the pool when I got a vision that I should, and I get to know that the Euphrates and the River Nile running all the way – the city carry everything." It was clear that Mother Nora was only comfortable with the pool when she could connect the pool to Africa. She made it clear that her work was the African way "because that is what I know". Bishop Jack made the observation that Mother Nora could now build her church because she has a pool. Mother Nora's site/church is named Mount Bethel Sacred Heart. Mother Nora's spiritual guide was Leader Wollery.

The African hut was Mother Nora's meeting house before the tent/church was set up. Now the African hut is decorated and used for special rituals. There is a centre pole, which is common in the more traditional Revival booth/church. The pole has different shelves with artefacts including replicas of African animals: lion, elephant and leopard. The tables, the bed and the walls are covered with African and African Jamaican artefacts, work tools, food and drinks. The hut is not a permanent structure on the site: it was made for Mother Nora's annual duty table. The duty was a four-night table. The third night was called Indian Night. The Indian King of Revival Bishop Wally Graham was on hand to celebrate the occasion with Mother Nora.

Difference between Seals and Symbols

1. Seals represent the core of the religion and cultural values that are central to the practice of the religion. They are relatively stable and their meanings are consistent in the ritual performances.
2. Seals represent the values of the system, and their meanings could be interpreted historically and through the indigenous and religious traditions of Revivalism. This makes them culture-specific.
3. Seals are typically fixed, meaning they are either a defined space or a fixed object placed in relation to special rituals – for example, the messenger seal. They are also the creation of the ritual specialist as sacred objects and spaces of power.
4. Symbols are not fixed objects or spaces like seals. They are objects that can be brought into play during the rituals and ceremonies as needed to fulfil a specific purpose.
5. Symbols are not as fixed in their meanings as the seals are; they must be interpreted according to the uniqueness of each ritual. The use of symbols, like the candle or the flag, in one ritual will carry a different meaning depending on the colour and how they are arranged in another ceremony. The meanings these symbols transmit will differ from ritual to ritual, hence it is important to observe how symbols are used.
6. Although symbols are important for day-to-day performance of rituals, they are not culture-specific. They are drawn from a group of available objects ritualized and given specific meaning.

Symbols

The organization of the Revivalist iconography is based on what the individual practitioners determine as seals and what they regard as symbols. Victor Turner, in his work on symbols, organized them into different categories, two of which are "dominant" and "instrumental". From my observations in the field, it is important to note that Turner's description of "dominant symbols" fits in with the characteristics of seals and the use of those icons grouped as symbols by Revivalists to that of "instrumental symbols".[9]

The symbols discussed below are used not only in Revivalism but also in the rituals and ceremonies of all the churches I visited. Colour symbolism is included here because colour in Revivalism has iconic significance.

The Flag

This symbol seems to generate much interest for the Revivalist. Every area or object for the Revivalist is justified in the Bible, and the flag is no exception. "Thou hast given a banner to them that fear thee, that it may be displayed because of the truth. Selah" (Psalm 60:4, KJV).

Flags were placed on all the sites visited. At Site 1 (Holt Close), they are placed on the altar and all around the church. At Site 2 (St. Michael's), there are two flags used at the entrance to welcome the people and to clear them from any evil as they enter the church. They are also used during the Revival ceremony to cut and clear. The colours of the flags are red and blue, but there are strips of cloth in red, gold, green, blue, pink, madras pattern, and white, hanging from the beams in the church on the walls. There are red, pink, white, gold and green flags. Site 3 (Gethsemane) has seven flags around its centre pole depicting the colours of the rainbow. The flags are used to entertain and greet the spirits. They are also used to clear the church and individuals from evil. Fabrics of different colors are kept in the church and used when necessary to meet the demands of the spirits.

Flags of different colours can be seen all across Jamaica on Revival sites as markers for both humans and spirits. Historically, the flag has been used in both Europe and Africa to symbolize the military, cultural identity, power

FIGURE 23. Flags used at a baptism – the red, green and gold flag represents all nations and the blue flag is the flag of Sacred Heart Church (2002)

and religious affiliation. It is evident that European flags were used by the Afro-Haitian people as objects of power and as models of local style, or "African-Haitian Aesthetic".[10] The flags used in the Morant Bay Rebellion and the red, green and gold flag used at Revival ceremonies are representative of African unity.

The Healing Jar

The healing jar was found on all the sites visited. This earthen jar of water, placed beside the healing table, is usually attended by a water messenger. At the sites visited, the healing jar is always set on a small table with glasses or mugs on the table. The water from the jar is given to those who take part in the healing ritual. It is believed that the water is touched and made ready for healing by the healing messengers. The healing jar is called a seal in some churches.

FIGURE 24. Site 1, healing jar (2002)

The Dove

The dove is a popular symbol in Revivalism. It was represented at all the sites visited and could be described as either a seal or a symbol. It is symbolic of the messengers and is associated with the biblical dove that took the message to Noah. The sign of the dove is not only visual but it is represented through sound and movement. A devotee can make the sound of a dove and move his or her arms like the wings of a dove during possession.

Flowers and Plants

Another symbol that seems to generate much movement when it comes into play is the floral arrangement, which includes blooms and greenery. At all of these sites, there were flowers, crotons and other plants. At Site 1 (Holt Close) there is always the croton. At Site 2 (St Michael's), the African basil is always present and used during the healing ceremony. The croton is also present. At Site 3, the croton and the rosemary plant are always present. At all three sites, flowers are brought in for the different ceremonies. At Site 4, the old site is covered with various types of croton.

FIGURE 25. Maria A. Robinson-Smith lighting a candle on the altar at the Sacred Heart Church (2004). (Clinton Hutton)

Candles

Candles are always present, especially at tables and other ceremonies. The candles are important in setting the order for the ceremony. The colours of the candles used and how they are arranged in numbers are important to the meaning and reading of the table. "The candles set the orders, the colour and the numbers and when the candles are not lit the orders are silent," Bishop Reid once said. The lighting of the candles at tables is referred to as the "lighting of the board". During the lighting of the board, money is collected for the lighting of each candle.

Water

Water could be described as the most important symbol in the church and is used for a number of things, including cleansing, healing and for sprinkling the seal during spirit work. Water is everywhere – in bottles, jars, basins, pools. There are many water rituals like baptism, sea table and river fasting. The white basin with water was a popular symbol at all the sites visited.

FIGURE 26. Site 6, basin of water (2005). (Clinton Hutton)

FIGURE 27. Baptism ceremony at Caymanas, St Catherine: the man in black trousers and blue headband is being baptized – note the position of his hands and the red, green and gold flag in the background (2002)

The Bible

The King James Version of the Bible is present in every church. It is used in interesting ways at different rituals, especially the table. When there is a four-pole table, four lessons are read – one from each side of the table. At most thanksgiving tables and on African night, seven lessons are read and, for each one, the reading ends at the seventh verse.

The Coconut

At all three sites, the coconut is placed under a table or in a corner, but standing ready for use if the need presents itself. The coconut is sometimes used for cutting destruction (diminishing evil).

Kananga Water

This scented water is also known as Florida water and is present at tables and used during the healing ceremonies. Whenever the Kananga water is opened and used, it gives off a sweet smell which always seems to add to the excitement of the event. Kananga water is used to wash away evil forces. The Kananga water and the aerated water (carbonated drinks) are found on all the sites. Beverages with alcoholic content, such as wine and rum, are not as popular but are always available and in close proximity to be brought into use upon request. When an alcoholic beverage is used, it always seems to bring on possession dancing.

The Drum

Drums are in all the churches. I observed that they are used during the first part of the ceremonies, especially during the warm-up activities. They are not used during the rituals held inside the church except for specific interventions, such as the entrance of a particular messenger. They are used in the ritual of bringing in the saints, which takes place the night before convention and after the breaking of the table on African night, in the entertainment area outside of the church. The drums are not used during the ritual of the 60, which is the most important ritual in Revivalism. The rattle drum and the bass drum make up the Revival drum set. These drums are played with padded sticks. Kumina drums (Kdandu and Playing Cast) can also be seen in some Revival churches; for example, those that celebrate African night.

Colour as Icon

The use of colour in Revivalism is important to the rituals and ceremonies. The colour of the candles, the flags and the tablecloth add special meaning to the occasion. Different events have set colours and the practitioners observe the colour code. At a Revival site or church there are flags of many different colours: red, blue, green, gold, pink, black and white. There is usually one flag with the colours red, green and gold. In some of the older churches like Leader Wollery's in St James and Mother Chris's (Christine Dennis) in Watt Town, there are seven squares of cloth in different colours: pink, blue, white, red, gold, green and purple. The flags most visible on any occasion will bear the colours representing the messengers most welcomed at that particular ceremony. For example, Miriam (guardian spirit) would be welcomed with the colour blue (in the form of a blue flag) and Michael (protector) with the colour red. Madras is also popular in the form of flags, tablecloth and bands uniforms.

Colour Cues: George Simpson versus the Present

Much of George Simpson's work on colour and meaning in his 1970 book, *Religious Cults of the Caribbean: Trinidad, Jamaica, and Haiti,* is still relevant. In order to get a background of colours and their interpretation, Simpson's colour cues will be matched with my findings on the use of colour.

Much of Simpson's early work on colour and the meaning of colour notes that the most important colours are white, red, blue and black.[11] Most of the people interviewed, especially in the 1970s, gave the same list. The colours gold, green and pink seem to have been added later. White was linked to purity and healing and was also a neutral colour that could be used for a crowning ceremony if the shepherd did not have a gold gown. White would work with the gold used in a waistband or in a headdress and possibly a shawl. White continues to be linked with purity and healing and is still the most popular colour used by ordinary members for dress in attendance at weekly services and meetings. The colours of the turban and accessories generally reflect the colours for the devotee's personal spirit or the purpose of the ceremony.

Blue

Simpson states that blue is the colour used for a conference with the ancestral spirits and for cooperation with all spirits. A blue gown is also used when contacting individual spirits. In 2002 this colour was described by Mother Morrison as the colour used for "intercession beyond the mercy seat". The colours used for the peace table set in Tivoli Gardens in 1979 were blue and white. The officiating bishops at this table were Bishop Carter Brown and Bishop Anderson. In my personal communications with Bourne and Hyatt Smith in 2003, the colour blue was described as highly spiritual; the colour can be used for healing and is the colour for a peace and love table. The blue flag was used at the table for Bishop Reid's healing in September 2001. "Blue is used to summon and bring the spiritual forces together, all good spirits", says Simpson.[12]

It would seem that blue has always been a strong spiritual colour and continues to be a colour that can rally the forces of the spirit world. It was noticeable that the blue used at the peace and love table was a different shade from that used at the healing tables. The blue used at healing tables was a deeper shade of blue.

Red

There are two popular shades of red: bright red and maroon or dark red. The red head-tie is used by the bishop or leader in rituals. According to Simpson, Reid and Bourne, this colour is a symbol of the blood of Christ. Red is used for cutting and clearing destruction or any evil. The cutting and clearing table could be spread with a red tablecloth or red and black tablecloth. The most featured candle would be red.

Red is a versatile colour. It was used in 1979 at a victory table held for the leader of the opposition Edward Seaga. The maroon red is representative of the Maroon heritage and is a popular colour for gowns. Bishop Reid uses it as his special dress. He describes it as his ancestral colour.

Yellow and Gold

Yellow and gold are often used together, as many Revivalists (the men in particular) do not seem able to differentiate between these two colours. Yellow is used for ordination ceremonies. Gold, says Simpson, represents the brightness of angels, while Elder DaCosta cites it as representing the source of power of the Holy Spirit. See figure 7, in which Bishop Bourne and the bands from the Zion Sacred Heart of Christ Sabbath Church are wearing gold headdress on his first visit to Watt Town after his ordination.

Green

Simpson links the colour green with growth in nature and understanding,[13] while Bourne associates the colour with prosperity.

Later Development of Colours

I observed a combination of red, green and gold in all the Revival churches I visited. This same combination of colours can be seen in the all-nation flag. Nearly all the groups that attended the first-quarter service at Watt Town in 2001 had an all-nation flag. The concept of all nations is one that sees Revivalism as representative of all of Africa and not just one group of Africans. These same colours are also known as the liberation colours.

At an upliftment table put on by Queen Esther, she wore a gown of gold, red, green and white. She refers to herself as a "Revival Bingy", thus linking the Revival movement to the Rastafari through the use of the colours and the fact that her hairstyle is dreadlocks. It is important to note that Queen Esther's husband is a Rastafarian who maintains a visiting relationship with the church. He is not a bands member and does not participate in the rituals.

Khaki and red, green and gold, brown and beige, and brown and orange are combinations used especially for birthday tables, ground tables and for the African order on African night. The colour combination most popular in the year 2001 among the bands at Watt Town were gold and green, and red and khaki. Revivalists associate the khaki and red combination with Michael, the warrior of the African order.

FIGURE 28. Queen Esther in her red, green and gold head-tie

There are variations in the creative use and meanings of colours by different bands, but there are also many constants. Most of the colours have not changed in interpretation since Simpson carried out his research in the 1950s, but some other combinations have been added. Colour continues to function as an icon in Revivalism because it represents and makes reference to things not seen.

Shared Orientations

Cultural or religious symbolism can only develop among individuals with shared orientations. Thus, Revival people are able to use their shared historical, social and African background to formulate conceptual representations of what they deem "really real". They have brought together a collection of objects that have special meaning. These symbolic productions represent for Revivalists those values and beliefs that are most dear to them.

The seals and symbols mentioned in no way exhaust the list of icons used in Revivalism. I chose to concentrate on the above-mentioned icons because they are representative of religious symbols recognized across the

Revival landscape. The seals may not look alike even when they fall into the same category; what is important is that they represent the same concepts. Ni Yarte makes the point that "once you understand the traditions you can move on".[14] In Revivalism much of the data is similar but there is room for personal data linked to individual experience and style. Hence, a four-point seal in one location will look different from one in another location but the conceptual representation will be the same.

It is in the rituals and ceremonies that the symbols come alive. The seals provide the spaces and the mood for ritual enactment while the symbols add meaning, colour, efficacy and excitement to the ceremonies. The seals and symbols form the core of the symbolic system that provides the knowledge that informs the ontology, aesthetics and world view of the Jamaican Revivalist.

CHAPTER 5

The Rituals of Revivalism
It's the Dance That Makes It Happen

The rituals and ceremonies of the church serve to articulate the Revival cosmology, and symbols make it possible for Revivalists to read, decode and interpret events in a similar way. These ceremonies take place in a number of churches across the island and it appears that the three most important ceremonies are tables, healing ceremonies and baptisms. Healing services are held weekly, baptism ceremonies when the need arises and tables are held all through the year whenever there is a need to celebrate or to make a request. These ceremonies are all important to the functions of the church but the healing ceremony/ritual is the most popular among members and non-members who share the Revival world view.

It is impossible to write about any area of Revivalism and not take note of the dance as well. The dance is an important element in all the ceremonies and rituals and it is also the outcome of some important rituals.

A Revival Table

Revival tables are held to facilitate communication with the spirit force. The union between man and spirit is important in the Revival cosmology, hence every effort is made to attract and bring the spirits to the ceremony. These tables are always colourful and of varying shapes. There is the regular rectangular table, the four-pole table, the ground table and other shapes depending on the occasion or the preference of the host.

Tables are popular because the Revivalist can always find something for which to give thanks, such as the birth of a child, a family member getting

FIGURE 29. Four-pole Revival table. (Clinton Hutton)

a job, a promotion, a gift from someone, a birthday, the recovery from an illness, being saved from an accident, a victory or deliverance from something. On the other hand, there are duty tables that are held for a number of reasons, such as someone being seriously ill, appeasing an ancestor, wishing for success at examinations or winning a court case.

Tables are always set on a seal whether they are raised or on the ground. How the table is set depends on the purpose of the table. These tables are set with candles, fruits, bread, flowers, cream soda and other items, and can be interpreted by the colours of the candles, flowers and the arrangements. The length of time it takes to set a table could range from a few minutes to days, depending on the ceremony. The regular healing or duty table would not require as much time as the annual three- or four-night thanksgiving table for the church. There is sometimes a feast table that necessitates the killing of a chicken or goat before the ceremony so that a blood sacrifice can be offered. The meat is prepared for the feast and the first serving is placed on the table for the spirits. A meal is served to the gathering after the table is closed.

Giving to the spirits so that they will serve you is, in short, what a table is about. This ceremony is popular because it caters to a wider gathering of people than just the immediate members of the church. Non-members can host a table for their needs. This allows for the belief system to be widespread among Jamaicans who are not necessarily devotees. It is deeply entrenched in the belief system that, at times, one must pay or give a gift to one's ancestors. This practice of offering libation or blood sacrifice before the building of a residence or business place or the preparation of a burial site is widely practised all over Jamaica.

The last night of the table is called African night. This could be the second night of a two-night table, the third night of a three-night table or the fourth night of a four-night table. On African night the people dress in African clothes. The table is sometimes set on the ground on or near a seal. At this kind of table, the singing and dancing is lively. The drums are used and the songs and dance include Maroon, Kumina, Dinky Mini and Bongo. The benches are pushed to the walls to make space. At Sacred Heart the tables are never held for more than three nights. On the last night after the breaking of the table, the bands move to the front of the church in the space defined by Bishop Reid as the entertainment area. At Gethsemane United Church (led by Bishop Hill), African night is always on the fourth night and it goes on all night in the yard in front of the church.

The most elaborate and ritualized ceremony that I observed was the fourth day of Mother Nora's table in Georges Plain, Westmoreland. At nine o'clock in the morning, a ritual ceremony was enacted by the all-nation seal in front of the African house. A goat was sacrificed amid singing, dancing and drumming, which lasted for nearly three hours. After this ritual, the preparation for the feast, which included the cooked goat meat and dumplings made from corn flour prepared on site, got into motion. At about 9:00 p.m., people started to gather. The duties for the table started around 10:30 p.m. These included Bible reading, singing, dancing and the lighting of the candles. After the candles were lit, Mother Nora and her party made their entrance. The procession started by circling the pole in the African Hut, then they went past the all-nation hut, the fire seal, and on to the messenger seal in the front of the yard. They circled the messenger seal three times with movement and song before entering the tent/church where they also marched around the table three times. At this point, Mother Nora was introduced and asked to bring her message by Leader/Master of Ceremonies Jonathan Williams. The table was exciting, with singing, dancing and people being touched by the spirit. It ended around half-past four on Thursday morning with a group of people possessed, singing and dancing. This table was well supported – the crowd that gathered was one of the largest I have seen at a table.

It is at these tables that the host and party give themselves over to the spirits from whom they seek special favours. The medium used here is the body. The success of the table is usually measured by the intensity and nature of the possession. When the host or members of the party become possessed, the body language displayed during the dance speaks to whether the spirit force is satisfied. There have been times when the host fails to satisfy the spirits and a repeat of another table or some special duty has to be performed to appease the spirits. The tables I have seen have been largely successful and provided the greatest opportunity for experiencing the interaction between humans and spirits.

Tables are held or can be held for a number of occasions. The reading can be serious or it can be for happy occasions. A red and black table could signify "cut and clear", meaning that there are some serious problems to be overcome either by an individual or by the group.

The combination of red and white could be symbolic of a love feast. Red and white candles set on the table with the duck bread, cream soda and fruits. Red and white (more red than white) also could be representative of a victory table. In 1979 Revivalists from across the island came together at Tivoli Gardens Community Centre to participate in dancing and singing in order to summon the spirit forces for victory at the polls for Edward Seaga in the forthcoming political elections in 1980.

It is at these tables that the use of icons is most visible. The ones most used are those to welcome and entertain the spirits and, importantly, to set the orders that give meaning to the ceremony. Bishop Reid states that "candles are used to set the orders"; he further states that the number of candles, the colours and whether they are lit or unlit all have special significance. With reference to the bell, he said: "The bell carries sound science. It takes you to the spirits." He further states: "The spirit world is big, no one thing can cover it." These things of which Reid speaks are icons that link the human to the spirit world.

Baptism

The baptism ceremonies were never held at the Sacred Heart Church or any of the other Revival churches that I attended. They are usually held at one of the baptism sites used by Revivalists. Many of the baptism sites have been in use since slavery and hold ancestral memories for the people who use them. They have, in the past, used the legendary sites such as Three Hole in Hope River (the home of a river mumma and the water spirits), Roaring River in St Ann, August Town and other legendary sites, but the present site for baptism is at Caymanas Estate, where the water flows from a mineral spring and is said to have healing properties. This ceremony begins in the church where those to be baptized take the vow around the centre seal of the church. The initiate or person to be baptized carries a cross around the seal three times – down the aisle of the church, around the water seal and back to the centre seal. He is surrounded by the leaders of the church and is given a candle and a Bible to hold while at the altar. After this ceremony, the procession to the baptism site takes place in the form of a motorcade with buses and cars because the place of baptism is miles away. In other parts of Jamaica, where the river or spring is within walking distance, the procession goes on foot.

At the baptism site, many different churches often gather on a Sunday morning with their members. Each church plants a flag or two in the water. One flag is the church flag and the other is the all-nation flag with the colours red, gold and green. The bishop or an elder (assisted by a water mother) enters the stream along with the flag bearers. At the entrance to the stream, the water mother keeps guard and also assists the person being baptized. Another water mother or water messenger leads initiates to the leader performing the ceremony. There is much excitement on the grounds with singing, dancing and waving of flags and banners. After the ceremony, those baptized are taken back to the church for a ritual around the seal. These baptism ceremonies can be held any time during the year but there is usually one before the annual pilgrimage to Watt Town so that the new members can be a part of that procession.

Baptismal ceremonies are very important to Revival people, especially the process of immersion. The person being baptized is dressed in white with a head covering. Before the act is performed, the palms of the initiate's hands are clasped before the individual is plunged under the water to rise up as a "newborn brother". After the baptism, they go back to church where the new converts are welcomed with much singing and dancing. They are then engaged around the seal in the act of spirit work.

Baptist leaders taught that "baptism by immersion not only washed away sin but conveyed an inner wisdom and knowledge that made it unnecessary to go to hear the white ministers".[1] Rivers and other bodies of water are important to the Dahomey and Asante belief systems. The establishing of baptism sites all across the island and the importance attached to these ceremonies, as evident in the support they get from the African Jamaican community, suggest a strong African connection.

The Healing Ceremony

The healing ceremony is one of the most-practised rituals in Revival. It includes not only physical but also emotional and spiritual wellness. This yearning for wellness is rooted in a cosmology that affirms harmony with ancestors, the spirit world and nature as important to the well-being of those living. Good health, good luck and success are sought after through everyday activities and spiritual journeys.

These ceremonies take place in different locations on special days of the week and at the same time of day each week. In one location, the healing rituals start at 9:00 p.m. on a Monday and end at midnight. In another, they begin at 3:00 p.m. on a Wednesday and continue to 6:00 p.m., occasionally going on to 7:00 p.m. In both these locations, special icons are used to acknowledge the presence of the healing messengers. Revivalists tell me that the healing messengers come in at a set time for these rituals. Upon their arrival, the church mothers and other attendants become very active with flags, flowers, water and other symbols brought into play to welcome or signal the presence of the spirits. During all this activity, the rhythm and dance remain constant and set the stage for the ceremony, providing the energy for its success. There are variations in how the healing ceremonies are conducted at each location but key elements are the same.

Description of the Rituals at Site 1, Holt Close

After attending these healing ceremonies for many years, I began to see that, amid all the excitement and multiplicity of mini dramas taking place simultaneously, the healing ritual had a set pattern. This ritual takes place around a table placed on the messenger seal. The seal is central to all rituals and ceremonies. The ritual proceedings could be divided into two main areas: the preliminaries and the official ceremony. The preliminaries include the greeting ritual, the scripture readings around the table and a short sermon. During the preliminaries, the gathering of people sing, greet each other and give short exhortations while they await the presence of the healing messengers. When the messengers appear, they are welcomed with "howdy-do" waving of hands, lifting of vase(s), singing and dancing. The ceremony begins officially with the devotees dancing and singing around the seal in an anticlockwise direction.

How the Rituals Are Organized

1. The robing: The leaders are robed in the ritual gown before entering the space designated for the ritual.
2. Cutting and clearing and "tun yu roll": The clients who have come for healing are cut and cleared in one instance by an attendant using a red flag and in the other instance by the use of a candle. Cutting and clearing and "tun yu roll" are mechanisms used to prepare the client.
3. The performance: The ritual leader works with his client, using the ritual mix (beverages), songs, rhythm, dance or any other methods he deems necessary to satisfy the needs of his client.

4. The coverage: One attendant stands behind the leader and covers the leader's back. This attendant also acts as a guide to the client going on to the next stage.
5. Healing water: The client is given a glass or cup of water to drink.

The Ritual

The bishop is robed just before he moves into the ritual space to prepare the ritual mix. The preparation of the ritual mix could include water, grapefruit, kananga water or any other ingredients requested by the bishop.

The candles are lit by members of the church hierarchy and invited guest(s). While the devotees dance around the table, the bishop prepares the mix, and those who have a role to play get into position. The clients are cut and cleared by an attendant before they enter the ritual area. In one instance a red candle was used, and in another instance a red flag was used.

At one site, the person going for healing stands with both arms stretched above the head. The attendant, using his left arm, passes the candle under the outstretched right arm of the client, then the left arm. The attendant uses his left arm to circle the client's left leg, the candle is retrieved with the right arm and then the right leg is circled. The attendant's right hand is used to circle the client's head and his left arm used to turn the client around. After "tun yu roll", the client is now ready to go to the bishop.

Bishop/Ritual Leader

The client is anointed or sprinkled with the healing mix by the ritual leader. During this phase of the ritual, the procedure depends on the need of the client and the leader's perception. When the bishop is through with the client, an attendant holds the client for a while, then send them over to the healing jar where the vineyard mother who is in attendance gives them a cup of water.

At another site, the basin is placed on a small table with five candles. The candles make a semi-circle and the basin is placed at the front of the semi-circle, which is the front of the table where the leader and ritual leader stand. A vase of croton leaves and a container with African barsley is also placed on the table. The table is blessed by the joining of hands across the table by the senior members of the group. A few people present are invited to light the candles. The leader calls for his assistants to take up their positions for the ceremony to begin. The clients are now in line, waiting for their turn to be healed. Along with the use of the flag, the client must "tun yu roll".

The second station is in front of the bishop and the healing table. At this station, the bishop (or "daddy", as he is called) performs the act of healing: using the ritual mix, he places some at different parts of the body with special emphasis according to the needs of the client. The next station is the armour-bearer who covers the bishop's back and also keeps an eye on the client. When the client is released by the bishop, this attendant guides them to the next station – the altar where there is a line of devotees who pray with the clients. The next station is the table with the healing water. Each client is given a glass of this water to drink.

Healing Dramas

In these ritual dramas, the bishop guides his client through a phase of liminality, and contact is made with the spirit world.

In one ritual drama at Site 1, a woman whose body has repeatedly been taken over by a male spirit comes to be rid of this spirit. The leader motions for the drumming and singing to stop. He begins chanting, repeating the words "tell him good-bye, tell him good-bye". He uses the ritual mix over her body. Then he calls for a bottle of cream soda and pours some over her head. The dancing continues. Two women who work with river spirits join in the dancing. They dance around her and with her. The leader invites a visiting bishop to join him. The choreography gets more intricate. There are now five main characters with the other devotees forming the chorus as the dancing continues. Two women get possessed and roll over, doing swimming motions on the floor near a basin of water. The leader and other members spray them with water from time to time. The bishop calls for wine, which he pours on the floor and on the client. The client becomes possessed and dances like a Kumina Queen. The leader dances with her like a Kumina King. He picks her up, dancing her around on his back for a few minutes. While she is on his back, she clasps her feet at the ankles and the form of her body takes the shape of a mermaid. After a few minutes of dancing, he places her on her feet and she continues dancing but now her dancing is not so erotic and painful but smooth and relaxed. The leader calls for a drink of cream soda and grapefruit for the client. After taking the drink, she is placed in a chair by two attendants.

At Site 1, in another ritual drama, a woman runs from the street into the healing ceremony. She moves towards the table. A devotee grabs her and leads her around the table in a clockwise direction before placing her in the line for healing, which was moving in an anticlockwise direction. During the singing and dancing, she becomes possessed. She falls to the ground, the leader calls for white rum, throws it on the floor, lights it with a candle and dances over the flames. The woman is taken up from the floor, held by some female attendants, and is made to dance. She dances as if being possessed by a ki-kongo spirit. As she dances, a group of devotees dance with her, imitating her movements. She regains her composure and is given a glass of water from the healing jar.

An important medium for these rituals is the dance. The entire ceremony is danced. It is quite unlike the laying of hands in churches, where there is stillness and a liturgy of words. Throughout this exercise, the rhythm and dances are continuous.

Analysis

Robing

The robing of the bishop is important in setting him apart from the rest of the members. It marks the first stage of the ritual process described as "separation". It signifies his authority and his wisdom. It is he who is most important in these ceremonies because the people rely on him to give the guidance necessary for the success of these rituals. What makes the ritual leader respected and qualified to lead? He must know and understand the ritual practices, the rhythms, the drills, the songs, the dance. But above all, he must be able to "see". Being able to see can be translated into being able to communicate with the spirits and to look into the future. A spiritual leader negotiates with the world of the spirits. When he is robed and he steps into the ritual space, it is as if he is transported to that space "betwixt and between".

Cutting and Clearing

Revivalists believe that there are always trials and tribulations that hinder the individual on both their physical and spiritual journeys. If one is to be successful, healthy and enjoy life, these hindrances need to be cleared from time to time. There is also the belief that there are good and bad spirits, and there needs to be constant negotiations with the spirit world so that the good spirits will ward off the bad spirits. Hence the many symbolic gestures of cutting and clearing and "tun yu roll".

The Performance

Victor Turner describes the performance as "the eye of the ritual". The ritual leader performs the roles of master of ceremonies, priest, producer and director. The ritual will be discussed here in two parts. The first phase is called a stable or structured ritual, during which the leader uses the ritual mix (a combination of water, fruits, leaves and sweet smells) embedded in a ritual setting with candles, flags, flowers and other icons. All of these icons add mystique to the proceedings. In this phase, the leader is in full control; he is the master of ceremonies for the proceedings. The clients are led by him and he goes through the process of anointing with the ritual mix as he is inspired to do. He is the artist and the performer as he leads the Revival bands with the right hymns, songs and liturgies. Most of all, he is the master dancer. He calls the bands the "chorus", which respond as he pulls on their strength and energy. He gives advice and instructions to his clients, loosens them up and relaxes them through the dance.

The second aspect of the performance is in keeping with those rituals when the leader comes into dialogue with the spirit world. In this phase, described by Turner as liminal, it is a performance not only with man and man but with man and spirit. It is his performance with the spirits, the fact that he can wrestle and communicate with them, dismiss them or use them at will, that defines his status as a master leader or a failed leader. It presents a picture of a scene that is relatively unstructured or anti-structured because it is outside of the norm. "If liminality is regarded as a time and place of withdrawal from normal moods of social action it can be seen as potentially

The Rituals of Revivalism

a period of exploring the central values and axioms of the culture in which it occurs."[2] These performances are informed by ancestral wisdom and bring to the fore ancestral experiences. The language, the rhythms and the dance, which at times are discernibly African-derived, confirm the sharing of ancestral knowledge. As Dona Richards puts it, "rhythm, dance and song are quintessential aspects of the cosmic African universal. Through them we participate in that universe and it is that participation which is continued in the diaspora and which belie the Fact of assimilation."[3] In this phase, the leader/producer/director pulls all the elements together by working through the sensory codes – sounds, visuals, touch, smell and taste – and combining them with ancestral wisdom, producing a blend that satisfies his client and allows for the continuity of traditions while leaving room for creativity and innovation. After this performance, the high point of the ritual has passed and the client is on the path back to the real world.

The Healing Water

All participants are given water to drink after a ritual. Revivalism is also a common-sense religion. After all journeys, spiritual or physical, people get tired and need to be refreshed. It is also felt that water is a cleanser and has healing properties.

Summary

The rituals demonstrate the Revival cosmology, as they bring into contact the living and the dead and allow for the ordering of the hierarchy. These rituals celebrate the union of man and spirit and actively facilitate that union. The icons and symbols, such as the water, flags, fruits, oils, beverages, perfumes, music and dance, all play a part in revealing or making manifest the spirits. The union also speaks to a world view where the spirit world is not separate from the human world. The spirits are very much a part of everyday existence and can be available to us if we understand and master the act of negotiating a safe setting for dialogue with that world.

Healing rituals and other rituals preserve the African legacy, mediate the struggles of a large number of people of African descent, and give release to their creative energies in Jamaica and the African diaspora. Equally important, they provide the communication system necessary for descendants of Africa to position Christianity within the African cosmological framework.

The spoken language from Africa may have been taken or lost but the body language speaks volumes. Through the body we have been able to get more than a glimpse into our people's history. Fragmented or otherwise, the dancing body has served to challenge foundation histories and to create openings for narratives of the past to inform the present.

Through practice and divine choreography manifested in the healing rituals, Revivalists have manipulated nature and the supernatural to address physical and mental disorders as well as other ills of society. The importance of rhythm and dance must be underscored because dance is the most important medium through which contact can be made to the spirit world. There are those who believe that the deep meaning of life is understood only by those who dance.

Iconography and Healing

At each stage of the healing ritual, the iconography is important to the structure and performance of the ritual. The physical space is organized so that different actions take place in different spaces. Bruce Mannheim describes this kind of spatial organization as a diagrammatic icon of the relationship in ritual responsibilities.[4] The space in the healing ritual is defined by the seal and the healing jar. The flags and the flowers are used to welcome the messengers. The blue and white tablecloth and blue and white uniform are the colours used to attract the healing messengers. The colour red is used to clear the clients of any evil and make them ready for healing. In some instances, it is a red candle, in others it is a red flag. The robing of the bishop is all part of the ceremony that prepares him to enter the ritual space for the performance of his duties. The symbolic movements of "cut and clear" and "tun yu roll" are also used to prepare the clients. The ritual mix is made up of grapefruit, leaves, and liquids. The grapefruit, some special leaves and liquids that include Kananga water, honey, and cream soda are symbolically linked to the process of healing. The rhythm and movement provide the energy for the performance of the ritual and facilitate the process of the coming together of the physical and spiritual world.

Performance Rituals and Ceremony

The rituals of Revivalism held in Revival churches, yards and ritual spaces are cultural performances that facilitate the expression of those philosophies and aesthetic preferences that are most important to the members of the group. It is through rituals that most aspects of a people's intangible heritage are transmitted from one generation to the next. Rituals are body-based practices, hence the physical aspects of the performances; how they are performed, when they are performed, who is involved and the relationship between the participants are important to the success of the ritual. Music and dance, two expressions of intangible heritage are not only enjoyed and practised by Revivalists but play a critical role in the effectiveness of their rituals and ceremonies.

Heavy rhythmic content and dancing are characteristics of Revivalism. Some of these rhythms and songs seem coded with special messages and deeper meaning and cannot be easily understood by an outsider. Some of these rhythms and movements are related to particular spirits and fill the gap when there is an absence of narrative or explanation.

In answer to the question, "How do you know when the messengers have arrived?" Pastor Queenie Brown gave the following response: "When the wind blows, you do not see the wind but you can realize that the wind is blowing because the tree is moving. This is how you can identify the spirits." Queenie is suggesting that it is possible for the messengers to be identified by the dance and the music.

The Healing Properties of Dance and Music

The music and dance connection is important to Revivalism because it provides the energy necessary to sustain the religion. It is believed that music and dance can restore health because it is through this medium that one is best able to connect and communicate with one's ancestors. Bishop Bourne spoke about the importance of rhythm and colour in attracting the healing messengers and he is convinced that with the right choice of rhythm health can be restored.

It is believed that there is a vital force that runs through all organic substance and it is connected to the spirit world, and that healers have the gift to manipulate these relationships through the use of music and dance. The popularity of Revival healers and healing ceremonies across Jamaica, especially among the youth, is a growing phenomenon. The demand for certain healers may be attributed to their skills in manipulating the music, song and dance complex. The appropriate choice of songs, rhythms and dances can provide access to the spiritual powers necessary to help their clients. Leaders who can access these powers are also rewarded financially.

Drilling the Bands/Blowing the Notes

The blowing of notes is an intense combination of music and sound used to lead and direct the rituals and ceremonies. All the leaders use the combination of music, song and dance. Connerton describes the blowing of notes as follows: "The rhythms of oral verse are the privileged mechanisms of recall because rhythm enlists the co-operation of a whole series of bodily motor reflexes in the work of remembrance."[5] The music, song and dance trilogy is very effective in spirit work. Seaga, in his poem "River Maid, River Maid", describes the music, song and dance correlation in spirit work:

> To the rockin of de body
> To the bowing of de head
> To the rhythm of the groaning
> The living dancing wid the dead.[6]

Dona Richards made the point that "it is not so much the meaning of the words which is important; it is the sound which makes the magic".[7] It is important to note that in nearly all the instances I witnessed, possession occurred during the drilling of the bands – not during the preaching. At a healing ceremony, a lady who was seated outside of the circle away from the drilling became possessed. I asked Pastor Queenie Brown how this happened; her reply was that "she heard a note, a key to which she must respond". Revivalists have used these rhythms over the years as a substitute for speech and to make connection with ancestral spirits. Through practices like these, they are able to gather information helpful in building links between African Jamaican people in the process of reclaiming their Africanness. The Revival leaders who lead the bands with the drills could be described as performing the function of the master drummer in an African context.

Nation Dance

The blowing of notes and the drilling of the bands is necessary for the dance ritual "Nation Dance" to take place. According to Patrick Taylor: "Anthropologically speaking, the Nation Dance is an Eastern Caribbean ancestral ceremony in which a community of people pays their respect to their ancestors and retrieves from them the knowledge of the past that will sustain the present and the future."[8] This ritual can also be seen at tables, healing rituals and sometimes at baptisms, vesper services and funerals in Jamaica. During this ritual, the bands journey through different "cities" while the leader blows the notes for the bands. The songs sung at this stage are drilling songs, not the regular hymns or choruses, with the group coming together in a tight circle (not all band members join in this exercise). The rhythms are led and directed by the leader. During this session the body language of the dancer reflects the dance of the "city" through which the bands journey. Bishop Reid and other Revival leaders use the word "city" in much the same way that Patrick Taylor uses "Nation Dance". As the drilling becomes more intense, the dance becomes more varied and exciting.

This series of rhythmic exercise or drilling of the bands allows the people access to ancestral knowledge. As the bands journey through the different "cities", it opens up the possibilities for the devotees to become possessed by the spirits of the ancestors of that city or nation. The healing ritual, table and Myal, or ritual of the circle, enforce and affirm the belief system of the community. The main intent of holding a table is to communicate with the spirits. The manifestation of this contact is usually through possession dancing. Hence at every successful table, there is much dancing because the main intent of these tables is ancestral communion. Spirit representatives of the nations of Africa and other spirits enrich the ceremony with varied possession dancing patterns. This kind of dance falls under the category of what Barbara Browning calls "divine choreography", when possessed individuals dance the choreography of the spirit.[9]

Possession dance is very important in religious worship and rituals because it is the dance that allows the individual to experience his religion to the highest level. Through dance it is possible for the devotees to cross over into the spiritual realms. It is the meeting point between the sacred and the secular, the creator and the created. Turner sets out the process of religious worship in three stages: the pre-liminal, liminal and post-liminal.[10] The pre-liminal stage is to prepare the devotees for higher worship and to invite the presence of the deity. The liminal stage is the process towards possession. It is during this stage that the devotees cross the human threshold to the realm of the supernatural. The post-liminal stage is that of reuniting the possessed with reality.

George Brandon, in his assessment of rituals, concludes that possession dances "are not a telling or a text but the performance of a world, its entities, powers and relations".[11] The greeting, its offerings and worship, the songs, dances, rhythms and the preaching are all pre-liminal preparation to the real climax of possession (the liminal stage), where the spirits take possession of the human body and perform through these bodies. Inger Sjørslev explains it as follows:

> The body becomes a social sign. When a medium is possessed by an Orixa, a gypsy, an old slave, a child spirit or an Exu, he or she, with his or her individual performance, is an element in a collective narrative, a common history that has to do with understanding oneself in the world. A ritual performance, in which the spirits are present, is thus at the same time for the individual medium a confirmation of personal identity, through the presentation of self, and a manifestation and reflection of the historical and social context within which the individual is placed.[12]

During possession, the individual assumes the mental and physical characteristics of some of these spirits who make up the pantheon of spirits for the religion. It is this process that allows the body to articulate the symbols and kinetic patterns of a particular culture or community. This is the art of embodied technique, where the body speaks for the individual as a confirmation of personal identity, animating symbolic gestures of cultural identity and modes of political and historical consciousness. This allows the dancer's body to act as a stage for the spirits to tell their stories. As the devotees dance in the spirit, the process facilitates the creation of a cultural text informed by a history from below. According to Linda Giles:

> Cultural texts are "written" and "read" by the society concerned; they are stories that the society tells itself about itself. Since the "language" employed is highly symbolic, it can associate many different levels of meaning and accommodate many different personal interpretations. Moreover it can reflect non-avowed aspects of society, which could not be stated through other means and actively restructure them into a metaphorical dramatic form. This form facilitates the affirmation of models of society that run counter to formal ideological statements without requiring public recognition.[13]

As Giles suggests, spirit possession provides an ideal medium for the production of cultural text. Through possession, Revivalists perform the dance of the spirits, experiencing fulfilment of their religion and access to ancestral wisdom. This process has also been described as a human transformation. Human transformation is the supernatural manifestation of a deity in the human body, wherein the body of the devotee is transformed into an icon or representation of the deity. During possession, the dance vocabulary and kinetic patterns represent the characteristics of the deity by which the human is possessed. It is during this act of possession that movements of spirits are inscribed on the body of the dancer. The body speaks that which cannot be said in words. These movements manifested during possession, along with movements taken from other rituals, form the core of the Revival iconography and, by extension, the Jamaican dance iconography. The dance iconography is an embodiment of the people's philosophy, hence the movement motifs and gestures are as important to the ceremonies as words to poetry.

The Revival Dance Iconography

The rituals and ceremonies of Revivalism are always rich with a variety of movement gestures, movement motifs and ceremonial dancing. There are, however, some gestures and movement motifs that are expressions of the Revival philosophy that are always repeated or performed by all Revival groups all over Jamaica. The movement motifs listed below form part of a system of meaning and representation through the dance. The 60 Step, wheeling, cut and clear, and "tun yu roll" are all movements that are representative of the Revival philosophy. Other categories of movements, form and structure are as follows:

- The Welcome Dance: a suite that resembles the quadrille
- Gestures: bow, curtsey, waving of hands
- Nation Dance: Bongo, Maroon, Indian, other nations
- Duty Movements: bell ringing, swimming, flying, chopping and clearing
- Percussion: clapping, stomping, moaning and a variety of other sounds
- Space Form: circle, semicircle, lines, procession, anticlockwise movements
- Other movements: balance step, swaying, shuffling, rocking
- Structure: set, improvisation, repetition
- Ceremonial dancing objects: The holding of objects in the hand while dancing, for example, the flag, flowers, machete and other objects

Photographs representing such movements were taken at performances of the rituals and ceremonies at churches and Revival sites all over Jamaica. Figures 30–34 show the dance motifs practised by Revivalists

FIGURE 30. Cut and clear, done while under Myal (2003)

FIGURE 31. Spin Me Dance (2004). (Clinton Hutton)

FIGURE 32. Wheeling (2003). (Clinton Hutton)

FIGURE 33. The Greeting Dance, at Site 1 (2003)

FIGURE 34. Two leaders greeting each other at Watt Town (2004). (Clinton Hutton)

During possession (figures 35–37) and Nation Dance (figures 38–40), the body becomes an icon representing the dance and culture of the spirit, the individual and the community.

FIGURE 35. Touched by the spirit (2004). (Clinton Hutton)

FIGURE 36. Mirroring the movements of the spirit (2004). (Clinton Hutton)

FIGURE 37. Duty movements – cutting and clearing (2004). (Clinton Hutton)

FIGURE 38. Indian Dance, Westmoreland (2004). (Clinton Hutton)

FIGURE 39. Indian Dance, August Town (2004). (Clinton Hutton)

FIGURE 40. Bongo, Westmoreland (2005). (Clinton Hutton)

Gestures are shown in figures 41–43 and figures 44–47 show characteristics of Revival/Afro-Jamaican dance: get-down quality, torso bent forward, soft knees, bent knees, angular elbows.

FIGURE 41. Wave: greeting (2004). (Clinton Hutton)

FIGURE 42. Bow and curtsey: interaction between man and man and man and spirit (2004). (Clinton Hutton)

FIGURE 43. Bow: the index fingers touch to form a V (2004). (Clinton Hutton)

FIGURE 44. Bent knees (2004). (Clinton Hutton)

FIGURE 45. The get-down quality (2002)

FIGURE 46. Motif from "London Bridge Is Falling Down", a ring game (2003)

FIGURE 47. Mother Chris at ninety-eight, dancing (2006). (Clinton Hutton)

The photographs in figures 30–47 capture some of the movement motifs that have been described in the text. Some of these motifs are linked to philosophical and supernatural activities. They also establish certain principles as to how humans relate to the supernatural force. The courtly behaviour demonstrated in the wave, bow, curtsey and the greeting motifs signifies welcome and respect to humans and spirit alike. The possession dancing gives an insight as to how the different nations come to dance. Two of the nations that were represented in the pictures were Bongo and Indian (see figures 38–40). Another important element in possession dancing is mirroring. In some instances, the possessed is controlled by another devotee, while in another the possessed is mirrored by another dancer. The act of mirroring allows for the dance of the ancestors to be learned and practised by the other devotees.

The Watt Town suite and the other motifs feature the main principles of Revival/African dance. The torso inclined forward, knees and elbows bent, parallel feet, the get-down quality, and the natural dance bend can be seen in the pictures. The dance suite also represents community, as the music making and the dancing in pairs and in groups bind people together.

Mother Chris, at ninety-eight years old in 2006, was still able to dance, conduct her healing ceremony and work the physician seal at Watt Town. Because she could dance she was able to experience her religion to the fullest. When one looks at the importance of dance to Revivalism and the people who practise it, one understands fully Bishop Reid's statement: "If I cannot dance, it makes no sense." When he turned down an invitation to attend the official opening of a branch of his church in Canada because he would not be able to dance, it was because he understood the importance of dance to the religious ceremonies.

Dance is one of the areas that best distinguishes Revival worship from all other religious forms in Jamaica. The dance may vary in the different ceremonies but it is always present. It has been described by some of my informants as a form of deliverance, healing, freedom, mediator and life. It is also the area that best unites us with our African past. The Revival dance iconography is a showcase of the dance legacy of Afro-Jamaican people. "To dance means to be alive. To be consciously alive means to dance," as aptly stated by a Luo chief (Kenya, 1964): "The deep meaning of life is understood only by those who dance."[14] One can only experience Revivalism to the fullest through dance. Revival rituals and ceremonies are a performance of our heritage.

Performance

Every good Revival leader is an excellent performer. This applies to Kapo, Reid, Graham, Walley, Rudd, Hill and numerous others known and not so well known. They are able to use singing, dancing, chanting and other rhythmic devices to bring the best out of their bands and to hold the bands together. They are also charismatic. It is not only the content of what is being performed, but also the quality of the performance that generates the power. Quality can be measured by their ability to engage the icons in uniting both humans and spirits during these performances.

What is special about all these Revival leaders or "master drummers" is that they have all been on spiritual journeys which took them away from day-to-day activities for days and sometimes weeks. During these journeys, they spent time in the counsel of the spirits where they were schooled in the techniques of spirit work.

Performance in Revivalism is twofold: it is the interaction between human beings and human beings, and it is also the interaction between human beings and spirits. "African-Caribbean worship is theatre, for the objective divine performance, in which pure and past spirits (as human beings are) together share the same stage for a few hours", wrote Chevannes.[15]

Revivalists have always used spirit possession as a vehicle for expressing their cultural identity and their concept of history. Through these cultural performances, Revivalists have recalled their history, recorded special events and emphasized community values, and through the constant repetition of preferred aesthetic qualities, they have performed an identity of difference.

CHAPTER 6

WATT TOWN
AN ICONIC SPACE

At **Watt Town the** processes that facilitate the retention of African patterns are documented through selected icons that span the Revival landscape. It shows how a people, through the use of their own cultural elements, can develop an identity of difference.

In this chapter, the more public iconic space at Watt Town is presented – its history, its mission, its physical setting, the people who use the shrine, their dress and accessories, and the spaces of power. I have compared the seals and symbols in form and concept with those of other churches visited. Having looked at the physical setting and icons at these churches and at Watt Town, the yearly pilgrimage to Watt Town was studied in an effort to understand what this journey means to the participants and how the icons are used to give clarity and meaning to the rituals.

How these spaces are used by individuals from across the island to communicate verbally and non-verbally is important in the tradition of shared meaning. It is also important to arrive at the true meanings as generated by the people's experience not only by what they say but also through gestures, body language and how they interact with each other to produce specific meanings. The interpretations given to certain objects or situations are sometimes different from those given by intellectuals or people from another culture. Hence it is important to know the meanings that the members of a group give to words, body signs and ritual objects.

I followed the activities of the bands from the Zion Sacred Heart of Christ Sabbath Church in Kingston on one of their visits to Watt Town in St Ann.

FIGURE 48. Sign erected in Watt Town in 2002

I call this journey an ontological journey, and it was organized in seven "portions". Each of the portions was enacted on a seal. I observed how the people interacted on the different seals, the songs they sang, the gestures they made, how they danced and the symbols used, because these things are important to a tradition of shared meanings.

Overview of Watt Town

Watt Town is a historical site. The late Henry Downer, who is said to have founded Watt Town in 1869, died in 1943 at the age of 105. The Watt Town institution or shrine has been operating for at least 140 years. Sister Cinderella (Mother of Seal) and Sister Thomas (Mother of Bands) are mentioned earlier than Henry Downer. This suggests that Watt Town's origin predates 1869. Downer's daughter Emily Downer ("Madda") was at one time also the spiritual head. Captain Will Wallace succeeded Henry Downer as head, and his son Phillip Wallace followed. Brother Henry Linton succeeded Wallace and "Madda" Josephs was next in line. She served as leader for many years until she became too ill to manage it and died in 2003. During the period of her illness and since her death, things have been held together by four bishops – Bishops Jack and Clarke from St Ann, Bishop Blake from Spanish Town and Brother Linton, who resides on the property. There is no problem among the four leaders about coordinating their days of worship. Bishops Jack, Linton and Clarke worship on Sunday while Blake worships on a Saturday.

There is a well-kept cemetery just beside the church where all the departed leaders have been laid to rest. This adds to the integrity of the site. According to authors Jacob Climo and Maria Cattell, "To those whose identities are centred in distant homelands the cemetery is memory space, a diasporic bridge which is a reflection of their homeland and an expression of collective experience."[1] Certainly, Watt Town is one of the oldest Revival sites in Jamaica. This institution has been sustained over the years not by any act of parliament or grants from any overseas governing body but by humble peasant folk – people from all across Jamaica. Turner's statement that people will always hold on to what is most important to them and that "it is through rituals that people express what is most important to their being and their strongest values" best explains this phenomenon.[2] I first visited this site in 1979 when I was a student at the Jamaica School of Dance, now the Edna Manley College, and on every occasion since then every parish has been represented.

Watt Town is a mission site strategically positioned on a hill offering a panoramic view of the surrounding hills and valleys of the parish of St Ann. It is a beautiful setting for a pilgrimage, the long uphill climb affording participants a scenic processional walk. The coming together of the different bands from all across the island with their colourful costumes and paraphernalia is a spectacular event. The singing and dancing and the waving of flags and staffs make excellent theatre for the onlooker. The mystique behind the opening and closing of the seals heightens the drama and speaks to the springs of energy and ancestral wisdom that can be accessed by those who, according to Bishop Bourne, understand the "notes and numbers".

Revivalists, scholars and interested observers visit Watt Town on the first Thursday of each quarter. The first quarter appears to be the largest gathering of the year. Thursday is Earth Day or Mourning Day for the Ashanti. On Mourning Day, one honors and gives reverence to one's ancestors. It is also a special day for the Congo people. One could interpret the practice of worship or mourning on Thursdays as a possible connection with the Akan heritage in Jamaica. The red, gold and green flag at the top of the hill highly suggests a connection between the rituals of Watt Town and the nations of Africa.

When one considers the offerings at Watt Town, it is easy to understand the level of preparation that is undertaken for the ritual journey. Some of the offerings include the sheer natural beauty of the place, a plateau surrounded by valleys filled with ancestral whispers (the seven seals); the coming together of pilgrims from all over Jamaica; the show of strength in numbers and workings of the bands; the uniforms of the bands with every one looking their best and wearing the colours as given to them by the spirit; a people dressed in a manner

FIGURE 49. Red, green and gold flag, Watt Town (2002)

that makes them feel good, their own mix of colours and styles complete with trimmings of cords, pencils, rods, staff, buttons, and "ric rac" braids, bringing along with them their gifts in kind – bread, fruits and various grocery items; and the people's talents in music, dance and oratory. The preparation and representation of self and community have all the necessary ingredients of a grand homecoming.

FIGURE 50. Bands bringing their gifts, Watt Town (2002)

Dress and Accessories

The most definitive element of Revivalism is the dress, which makes a strong visual statement. It is at Watt Town that dress makes a magnificent statement as the bands come with their different designs and mix of colours from all fourteen parishes. They come not to compete but to look their best. Dresses include accessories and hand-held items in colour combination. The colours, the styles and the accessories combine to make a striking impact. The combination of strong primary colours and the colours of the rainbow are popular. Combinations of red and blue, black and yellow, red and white, purple and white, pink and white, and green and gold are still very popular. There is also khaki, some with red and gold, and green and gold combinations.

The Turban

In the words of Bishop Robert Clarke, the turban "is our spiritual emblem. The number of pleats in the turban tell you the orders you are under, so it is very important to the message and the activities." Bishop Robert Clarke grew up in the Baptist Church but at the age of fifteen he answered the call to Revivalism in Watt Town. He is the founder and bishop of the United Holiness Church of Christ in Gibraltar, a district in the parish of St Ann. He is also the overseer for twenty-one churches in different parts of the island. Bishop Clarke is respected in his community and represents his parish as a justice of the peace. He does not wear a turban all the time, but whenever he is conducting a ritual, a spiritual activity or working the seals at Watt Town, he wears a turban.

FIGURE 51. Bishop Robert Clarke in black, blue and red turban, and Bishop Eric Guthrie in blue, khaki and red turban. (Clinton Hutton)

Bishop Clarke said the turban is important to the religion because it is fixed to the numbers you are under and gives meaning to the ceremony. He went on to say that the pleats and the colour of a turban represents different messengers; for example, red and khaki represent the authority orders, and the bandana represents the all-nation orders. He further stated that he and Bishop Eric Guthrie are always under the authority orders at Watt Town and that they hold all the keys at Watt Town.

"We take the turban very serious, we do not wear it everywhere," Bishop Clarke said. "It is worn when we are on mission, the material used to make the turban should be cotton or linen. It should not be washed with other clothes, it is set apart."

Revivalists all across Jamaica wear turbans and it is that which best distinguishes them from the members of other religions. At Watt Town, the turban appears in different mixes of colours and styles, but what is most stunning is the eminence it gives to the leaders, especially the male leaders.

Head Turbans

The headdress (turban), whether worn by a male or female, is probably what is most unique about Revivalists. They take great pride in preparing these wraps, and they manage to keep the identity of their bands while expressing their individuality. The head wrap becomes an extension of the head, and the style and colour combination serve to accentuate the movements of the head. The colours chosen can be associated with either group meaning or individual choice. The headdress or turban, though attractive, is not just

FIGURE 52. Turban. (Clinton Hutton)

about style but about power. "If the angel did not give you your turban, it is powerless. It is about the power of the angels," said Bishop Guthrie.

FIGURE 53. Turban.
(Clinton Hutton)

FIGURE 54. Head-tie with seven colours.
(Clinton Hutton)

Accessories

The accessories are all symbols representative of spirit work. Scissors are used to reduce destruction, and the pencil and book are used to take the message. The Bible is a Christian symbol and the croton a symbol of African spirituality. A new addition to the list of accessories is now the cellular phone. It helps to keep Revival people in touch and it has become part of the Revival network.

The dresses allow for freedom of movement – outstretched arms, rotation of torso, turns and tilts. Here the chosen styles are those which favour pleats, flair, bias and gathers for the women and robes for the men. The dress can be described as concealing the body. The bodies of both the men and women are usually well covered. For the women, long sleeves, long skirts and head wraps are indispensable features of the dress code. The dress, headdress, and accessories are visual symbols that distinguish the Revivalists from people of other religions. The style of dress not only makes the Revivalist visible but sends messages that speak to the Revival cosmology.

FIGURE 55. Young leader from August Town, armed with pencils and notebook to receive the message, Watt Town (2003). (Clinton Hutton)

FIGURE 56. Leader with both the Bible and the croton leaves close to her heart, Watt Town (2003). (Clinton Hutton)

The Watt Town Message

"People come to pick up their 'portion' to build up themselves," said Bishop Guthrie. "Watt Town message is not an evangelist message, it is a portion message where people come to pick up their numbers and their orders from the angels. In order to carry 'portion message' you have to be able to respond to the key with the right numbers. When you touch the key, someone will get touched. If you do not have a key, you cannot open the door. It is the letters that give the leadership." Guthrie went on to explain that if you do not know the system of keys, letters and numbers, you cannot be a leader. The understanding of this system is imperative if one is to access the knowledge and wisdom from the seals or spaces of power.

The Spaces of Power

The bands begin their official procession at the first seal, which is described by Leader Edgar Linton as the Sunday School seal. Then they start the climb around the old seal, one of the first established at the site, which is like a circle. One must circle this seal in order to get to the steps that lead to another seal. Upon reaching the steps, the visiting bands are met by the leader designated to preside over the ceremony. The leader of the visiting bands says a prayer when the bands are in place. After the prayer, they are welcomed to climb the steps and to circle the seal referred to as the "office" by some members

FIGURE 57. Mother with rod ruler and cellular phone leads the incoming bands around the seal, cutting and clearing (2003)

or the "sign in" by others. Here all visiting bands are led around the seal by the leaders, singing and dancing usually, doing the 60 Step.

FIGURE 58. A spiritualist marking the seal at noon (2002)

FIGURE 59. The message room with the gifts collected from the bands across the island (2002)

On this welcome seal, all bands sign in on arrival and sign out on departure. On one side of the seal is a four-point pole and on the other side is the message room. After signing in on this seal, the bands are led into the church. "Come in with your number", they sing. It is typical for them to sing a chorus or a Sankey (hymn) as they enter. The ceremony breaks to accommodate the introduction and greeting by the rest of the congregation and a short message or exhortation from the leader of the incoming bands. By about 10:00 a.m. there is no more room in the church, so some of the bands go to work on the seal or to refresh themselves among the trees or just find a space where they can enjoy the singing, dancing and exhortations.

A space much sought after by visiting bands is the physician seal. This is a seal that is worked by a number of bands for empowerment and is used especially by those who work with the healing messenger. It is located to the left of the healing room. There are a number of signs on this seal and on a wall close by. After the Sacred Heart bands worked the seal along with two other churches for about two hours, the leader of the session, Bishop Bourne, commented, "We have all received individual blessings here. We have received our own blessings and we must use these blessings even if is only one we get."

FIGURE 60. Two leaders sharing space on the physician seal (2003)

There is also a seal inside the church in front of the altar – the messenger seal. On this seal, different bands bring their problems or concerns to be worked out with the help or involvement of members from other bands. The pilgrims seek individual healing or empowerment in this space. For a healing ritual, the basin of water with herbs is usually placed on a chair or on the seal itself. When leaders are being empowered, the devotees encircle the seal. They sing and dance in response to the blowing of the notes by the leader.

At about 3:00 p.m. bands start to sign out. This is a lengthy exercise because each band must form a queue to go into the message room. This room is in one of the first structures built on the site, with its own seal. Prayer is then said as the bands circle the seal, singing and dancing. During this exercise each member receives a blessing or a gift. Then they leave the message room to sign out at the office/seal. The bands, led by one of the Watt Town elders, circle the seal three times, then make their exit down the steps and down the hill for the journey home.

FIGURE 61. Collecting the message (croton leaves) from the garden (2003)

FIGURE 62. Preparing the message and blessings for the bands (2003)

FIGURE 63. Bands lining up to do the final ritual and to receive their blessing (2003)

FIGURE 64. Bands returning home with their blessing (2003). (Clinton Hutton)

The Cosmological Ordering of Space

The spaces at Watt Town provide areas for people to dance. The welcome seal is called the office because the practitioners sign in on this seal. This ritual could be compared with the registration exercise at a conference. This seal also functions as the deliverance seal after 12:00 p.m. It is the largest space for movement on the compound. There is space for those who are doing spirit work or dancing and for those who watch from the sides. The physician seal is another large area where the bands actively work. It is a wellspring for those in the healing ministry whether physical or spiritual. The message seal inside the church is the largest area in the small and usually packed church. Here different groups get a chance to dance and greet each other. It is also a space that allows for the working through of difficult problems and the empowerment of leaders. The four-point pole is the first symbol that greets one on entering the office. These seals therefore provide the space where different messengers come to share with humans. They come at different times during the day. Bishop Bourne made reference to the fact that time was important to the work, as certain messengers appear at different times; groups of people will leave the church to work with the messengers who have arrived on the deliverance seal at about 12:00 p.m. There are a number of messengers who bring different skills and perform different functions in these spaces. Many of the symbols seen in other churches could be seen at Watt Town – the flag, the writing on the wall, groves of crotons all around and a few candles – but it is the seal that takes centre stage at Watt Town. The cosmology is encoded in the spaces at Watt Town.

Watt Town: An Ontological Journey

Having looked at the physical setting and icons at churches in different parts of the island and at Watt Town, I now turn to the yearly pilgrimage to Watt Town in an effort to understand what this journey means to the people and how the icons are used to give clarity and meaning to the rituals. I followed the activities of the bands from the Zion Sacred Heart of Christ Sabbath Church on one of their visits to Watt Town.

Here I will focus on one specific pilgrimage to Watt Town by the bands in an effort to get a glimpse into some of the happenings that have made the Watt Town experience so important to Revivalists. I call it an ontological journey because this journey is so important to the people, their sense of being through their religion and their world view. Following this discussion, I will look at the seven portions of Watt Town as experienced through the ontological journey of the bands. Each of the seven portions takes place in a different space, except portions 2 and 5 which take place on the same seal but at a different time of day.

The seven portions of Watt Town are as follows:

- Portion 1: The Preparation
- Portion 2: The Signing
- Portion 3: Working the Order

- Portion 4: The Revelation
- Portion 5: The Meeting of the Powers
- Portion 6: The Blessing
- Portion 7: Working the Message

Portion 1: The Preparation

Nearly three months before the event, one the members told me that the colours to be worn to Watt Town were khaki and gold. The colours were decided by Bishop-elect Bourne, who resides in Toronto. He said the colours were revealed to him "not in a dream but through the thought process, from the inspiration of God". Another member told me that she also got a vision of khaki but it was teamed with red, green and gold. Members were allowed their individuality with the design and mix of colours. The individual members went about getting their material and choosing their design. All the bands wore khaki and gold but some members had a touch of red or green lace, braid or bias binding around the hem, neck or sleeve of their dresses. Men's garments were plain for the most part but some were decorated with cords. The uniformity and oneness were shown by the colours of the bands.

Two members of the church were in charge of arranging transportation, collecting the fares from the other members and securing a bus for the journey. There was much anxiety among the brethren due to the ill health of the bishop of the church. It was the first time in forty years that a new bishop would be leading the bands to Watt Town. There was also some reservation about the choice of Bishop-elect Bourne, who had started another branch of the Sacred Heart Church in Canada but came back to Jamaica to lead the church on the pilgrimage. The old bishop was taken on the journey as well, although he had to be carried by male members of the church.

The first stage of the ritual took place on the seal around the message table in the home church in Kingston. At 5:00 a.m. the pilgrims gathered at the church, where they circled the message table, prayed and sang hymns such as "My Times Are in God's Hands".

The brethren were anointed with consecrated Canadian Healing Oil by the bishop-elect during the singing and movement around the seal. After the anointing of the people, the bus was consecrated for the journey. Water was sprinkled in the bus, green bush passed through the windows and all through the bus, and the flag mother "flagged out" the vehicle. After the cleansing of the bus, there was prayer inviting the guardian angels to pilot them safely and to carry them through the journey. Having completed this procedure that the brethren have followed for years, they mounted the bus at 6:30 a.m. for the journey, singing, clapping and drumming all with the same focus. "It was a happy trip. The brethren sang, clapped and rocked with the rhythm from Kingston to Watt Town," reminisced Bishop Bourne.

Portion 2: The Signing

The bands arrived at Watt Town at about 9:30 a.m. A number of bands were already on the site. The bishop-elect gave the orders for the brethren to get in line, in preparation for the procession.

Things were not as orderly as they were the previous year. Although the young bishop-elect had journeyed from Canada to lead the bands, the presence of Bishop Reid (who was not physically able to lead the procession) created some confusion in the minds of the brethren whose view was that "not because him sick we can't dash him wey". Bourne was quite a diplomat and eventually was able to lead the bands without rancour. He called the bands together, raised a song and led the procession up the hill to the entrance of the seal.

He beckoned the bands to stop and wait until the retired bishop, who was being carried, was taken onto the seal. The bands sang and danced during the waiting period. Bishop Reid was welcomed to the seal by the presiding masters of ceremonies or bands masters. He was then taken and seated in the church. After the retired bishop was accorded the welcome and respect due to a chief, Bourne was also welcomed before he took the bands through the ritual of signing in.

The order of the procession around the seal was directed by the two bands masters, Bourne and the senior members of the bands, followed by the ordinary members. They circled the seal anticlockwise three times, singing and dancing as they went around. Gifts were then presented to the host, Watt Town. Sister Millie accepted the gifts on behalf of Watt Town.

After the signing in of the bands, Bourne brought greetings and salutations to the congregation in the already-packed church. This section of the proceedings took about fifteen minutes. The bands then left the church to clear the way for other bands.

Portion 3: Working the Order

The next portion was "working the order", or "working the spirit" on the physician's seal. "The healing angels tarry on this spot and our church is a healing ministry so we station on this seal to interact with the healing messengers," said Bishop Bourne. The bands danced, sang and made rhythmic sounds for at least two hours. Some of the songs that were sung on this seal were "Bright Morning Star", "The Angels Have Arrived to Sign My Name" and "Bongo Man". One of the songs that caused much excitement was "Don't You Trouble Zion". Bourne, assisted by the spiritual leaders of the bands, took them through different drills. He was assisted by the bands mother and two evangelists, one male and the other female.

At times the drills would stop to facilitate the entrance of different messengers. Each time the rhythm changed, the body attitude of the participants also changed. The body attitude sometimes indicated or signalled for a change of rhythm. During the period there was the blowing of notes. This was rhythmic and accommodated all kinds of sounds. The rhythmic movement of the body assisted in the creation of sounds and the synchronization of movement and sound. The participants repeated the same movements over and over, sometimes changing their body stances or moving anticlockwise in a circle. While the rhythmic movement and the basic steps were constant, individuals sometimes added their own touch or variation.

There were times when an individual, usually one of the leaders, would move to the centre of the circle, do a variation on the movement or change the movement. The others would either imitate the movement or just continue to keep the rhythm. At other times, the leader would mimic the actions of the initiator while the bands stuck to the 60 Step which is regarded as the basic movement.

At different points of the drill, individual members would get in the spirit, being stuck on a particular movement or a gaze – eyes fixed on an unseen object, making mimetic gestures. The rest of the bands would work with them through the journey. There was much energy and power circulating in the group – stepping, trumping and rhythm making. At the end of this drilling session Bishop Bourne made the following comment: "We were replenished and strengthened through communicating with God and the messengers." This session was spiritually uplifting even for the onlookers. The dancing, rhythms, singing and the spirituality of the people were at a peak. Bishop-elect Bourne then signalled the band members to break their fast. The serving of bread and water took place on the seal, which seemed to have also facilitated the inclusion of "the unseen".

Portion 4: The Revelation

Take Your Lantern

After lunch, the brethren gathered in the church at a space in front of the table. Bishop-elect Bourne brought a short message to the members, thanking God for His mercies. The gathering then sang the hymn "Your Grace and Mercy Have Brought Me Through" in the regular long-metre Revival style. Two women circled the old bishop on bent knees with hands moving up and down. The members of the congregation from other bands joined in the singing, with one woman tracking the words of the hymn. The rhythm changed as Bishop Bourne started blowing the notes and the bands members began to dance. A spiritual leader from another group led the dancing and assisted in working the bands through their labour. His arms moved as if he were on a journey and had to clear the way.

They went from singing to humming to "trumping". The bands danced around Bishop Reid, rocking, trumping and circling him. Assisted by one of the female members, the head wrap of the bishop-elect was removed and tied around his chest. He handed a lantern to Bishop Reid, then poured water from a bottle to wash the bishop's face, hands and feet. After drinking water from a bottle, he gave Bishop Reid the bottle so that he could also drink from it.

At this point, the dance became more intense. A spiritual leader from another band took centre stage with knees bent and torso bent over towards the ground, arms moving up and down, out and in to the rhythm, bowing and groaning as he led the bands through their journey. The dancing and rhythm were rich, with the members moving around and encircling Bishop Reid. Bourne, who was leading the ceremony, lifted the bishop to his feet and changed the song to "A Wonderful Saviour Is Jesus My Lord". He then signalled the male members to help the bishop leave the church. All the members were ordered to gather their belongings and line up for the next phase.

The original Zion people (those who were more 60 than 61) began to look uneasy. The order seemed to have crossed the line. The rhythm, dance and sounds were being interpreted by some as 61, which is at the African end of the continuum. Some Revivalists who see themselves as original Zion/60 are not comfortable when the practice becomes more African/61. The bishop-elect raised Bishop Reid to his feet and started a new song. There was a paradigm shift. The church was once again at ease.

Portion 5: The Meeting of the Powers

In Revivalism there is always room for spontaneity, as during the day members of the bands interact with other groups. After leaving the church, there was a mixed group already working on the deliverance seal. The singing was led by a young master singer from a church in Savanna-la-Mar, who was also a good dancer. During this session, different band members came together in what appeared to be a show of power, or a clash of the giants. At points, it was like the ring game motif of "Show Me Your Motion". Bishop-elect Bourne went in and "showed his motion". One band brought a black cloth that members used to create an inner circle. A leader explained the use of this cloth as an act of deliverance. During this deliverance exercise, pieces of different colored cloth were brought into the circle at the request of the messengers. As Bishop Bourne explained, there was some disturbance on the site and clearance was necessary. The bishop had difficulty getting his members to move from this activity, as everybody was dancing and singing. The dance was dynamic and electrifying, bringing out the strength and energy especially of the men. It was a fitting finale for the day's activities.

Portion 6: The Blessing

Bourne led the bands to the message room, where the leader in charge of the message room, Major Linton, prayed and asked for God's blessing on the bands and for journeying mercies. The bands then circled the room anticlockwise and each member was given a blessing in the form of a branch of croton that was consecrated. This signified a spiritual message. Bourne received his individual message and a package from the church.

It is customary for the bands, led by the bishop in charge, to sign out around the seal but because of the large gathering on the seal, there was no space for the anticlockwise circling on the seal. It had to be done in the message room, where the bands signed out and started down the hill for the journey home.

Portion 7: Working the Message

The spiritual gifts and messages received in the message room were taken back to the church in Kingston. "The church will work these orders for the rest of the year," said Bishop Bourne. On the first Sabbath after the journey to Watt Town, the retired bishop, the bishop-elect and the full bands, strengthened, refreshed and energized by the journey, worked the message on the church seal. In an interesting ceremony, the bands formed a circle around the seal, singing and trumping the 60 Step. The bishop then placed a branch of the croton in a basin of water on the table. He also gave each member a piece of croton leaf and they were asked to share with the congregation what the journey to Watt Town meant to them. Some members spoke of the blessings they received and the goodness of God. One woman in describing her experience said, "It feels like bubbling fire." An interesting ritual drama then took place between the bishop-elect and one of the mothers as they danced for about forty minutes. Sometimes they mirrored each other's movements, sometimes it was action and reaction while the bands sustained the energy with rhythm and dance. A few members were touched by the spirit and one woman was possessed. The bands sang and danced with her on her journey. After that exercise, the bands laboured in the spirit, singing and dancing. One of my informants told me that the seal had to be closed in order to end the ritual.

Analysis of the Seven Portions

In portion 1, leaves, flags and Canadian Healing Oil have to be iconized and made into ritual objects imbued with meaning. These icons were used to transform the bus into a ritual space. The rituals both on the seal and in the bus gave the members a feeling of well-being and the right mood for the journey. They could be classified as rituals of spiritual union and well-being. The concept of the circle suggests unity and continuity. The ancestors are part of the circle and they can be reached when needed. Trumping and labouring while circling the table was an invitation to the spirit force.

Portion 2, the signing in, is one of the most important rituals at Watt Town and it takes place on the welcome seal or office. It provides a space for individuals to keep in touch with and honour their ancestors. The practice is reciprocal: we honour and bring gifts so that we may be served in return physically or spiritually (see figure 50). This ritual fits into the category of ancestor communion and respect, or ritual of respect, as categorized by Richards.[3]

It is on this seal that cutting and clearing is most practised. It is also the official entry for the bands, and those who need to be cleared or delivered are cut and cleared by the Watt Town bands mother or leader (see figure 56). Simpson mentions the cutting and clearing table as observed in Morant Bay as follows, "the purpose of which is to set a power to get away from trouble".[4] Karen McCarthy Brown opines that the theory of binding and loosing is at the heart of Vodou philosophy: "In order to get things flowing among persons and between persons and spirits, gates have to be opened, pathways cleared, chains broken, blockages removed and knots untied."[5]

The cutting and clearing in Revivalism is central to its philosophy. All across the island this term is used. In response to cutting and clearing is the "tun yu roll". Richards suggests that it is this kind of philosophy "that remains the indomitable strength of a people plagued by political power-lessness".[6] This act continues to be a source of power for those who believe in the cutting and clearing.

Portion 3, working the order, can be classified as a healing or, more precisely, a ritual of empowerment. Power and knowledge were sought from the healing messengers on this seal. The rhythmic drills, blowing of notes and dancing were used to invite and welcome the messengers. As the bands journeyed through the orders, each different encounter was mirrored in the movements and rhythm but the basic dance step was the 60 Step. In a lecture on Caribbean culture, Chevannes made the point that, in his view, this group of rituals was about the acquisition of spiritual power. He continued: "By knowing how to harness spiritual powers, one is able to master the present life, uphold one's interest, subordinate one's enemy, thwart his machinations and control others."[7] Every time someone was touched by the spirit they would erupt with dancing and sounds. The action on this seal and the sharing was like a spiritual communion that empowered the participants. As Bishop Bourne stated, they were replenished and strengthened through communicating with God and the messengers.

Portion 4, the revelation, took place inside the church. Repeatedly the paradigm shifted from Europe to Africa. The songs sung were reflective of the Christian church, but slowly the songs inched along the continuum. The rhythm strengthened, the words swallowed, the preaching ceased, the bishop-elect stepped aside, Bishop Reid blew the notes, and a leader/dancer from another band took centre stage. Through actions of "a mindful body", Bishop Reid played the roles of mediator, harmonizer and griot. The people

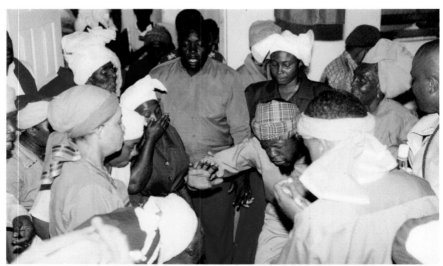

FIGURE 65. A leader from another band working with the bands from Holt Close, cutting and clearing (2002)

responded with the appropriate body attitude, and the dancer cleared the path for the bands to come together in unity.

After observing these rituals, it was clear that the congregation had just witnessed the spiritual sanctioning of Bishop Bourne. The washing of the old bishop's hands and feet was symbolic and multilayered in its meanings. One could interpret it as a healing ritual because his health was in a precarious state. But it was also similar to the Christian ritual of Passover, when Jesus handed over the ministry to his disciples. The bands, dancing anticlockwise to the 60 Step, followed by the "bessy down" movement with the pelvis leading, circling Bishop Reid, suggested a connection with the ancestral force. When I asked the bishop-elect about the dance during this session, which was characterized by soft knee, hips rotating, torso leaning forward and feet close to the ground, he replied that "the dancing was making intercession with the spirit to be merciful and continue to strengthen the bishop".

The use of the lantern was also symbolic, especially because it was a daytime event and was not needed to provide light. "I used the lantern to interact with the bishop; even though he is sick, he is still the chief leader. The spirit led me to interact with him because he had certain knowledge and authority that had to be passed to me. In the Bible, Elijah passed the baton to Elisha, passing from the older bishop to the younger."

Bishop-elect Bourne is an intelligent man. On watching his performance, I was reminded of Jamake Highwater's statement: "Ritual is not performed by primitive people but rather, it is produced by all peoples still in touch with the capacity to express themselves in metaphor."[8]

I could not understand why the ailing bishop should want to endanger his life by travelling over eighty miles from Kingston to Watt Town, but by the end of this segment it became clear to me what this journey meant to him. He had made this journey every year for forty years. Now in the winter of his life, he was faced not only with a crisis in his health but with the transference of leadership, which was so crucial to the stability of the church that he had established. If there was to be a resolve, one sanctioned not only by him but by the supernatural powers, why not at Watt Town?

There were no great speeches, no charters or bills of rights, but through songs, rhythms and dances, many profound statements were made. The song chosen by Bishop-elect Bourne on the seal of his home church, "My

Time Is in Your Hands, Lord", was his way of committing himself to the task, knowing that he had done all that was required of him and the rest was now out of his hands. The second song raised by the church mother on the physician's seal, "Don't You Trouble Zion", was a statement regarding her faith in the decision of the old bishop and her allegiance to the young bishop. It may be just coincidence that the church mother is ruled by Miriam, the guardian spirit of the home church.

Upon leaving the physician's seal, Bourne started the song, "Your Grace and Mercy Brought Me Through". This was sung in many styles, from the traditional Sankey to a rhythmical version, but there was a sense of accomplishment and satisfaction.

At the end of the ritual, in the portion called Revelation, the song "A Wonderful Saviour Is Jesus My Lord" was raised by Bourne. The words of the chorus seemed to have special meaning:

> He hideth my soul in the cleft of the rock
> That shadows a dry thirsty land
> He hideth my life in the depths of his love
> And covers me there with his hand.[9]

With this song, Bourne seemed to be expressing confidence that the resolution had come and that he had received the blessing to take up the mantle. Songs, rhythms and movements were also used to change the "order" and put the original Zion members at ease.

Portion 5 brought together band members from across the island, who were singing, dancing, and using different colours and symbols to bring in the messengers. The leaders took turns in blowing the notes for this session. This suite was a display of the common elements – like the Myal circle, moving anticlockwise around the circle, blowing the notes, the 60 Step, and the use of colours and different symbols – that have held Revivalism together across the island. The coming together of Revivalists from across the island in song, rhythm, dance and dress was a powerful display of African aesthetics.

In portion 6, the circling of the seal, the receiving of the gift of croton leaves was an act that was symbolic of Revivalism in the same way that the breaking of bread and sharing of wine is symbolic of Christianity. The gift of croton leaves is the symbol of African spirituality. This gift was received by participants, who took the leaves back to their home churches for a communion on their church seal. This exemplifies how the network is maintained across the island.

During all seven portions of the ritual, the icons were used to clarify and give meaning to the rituals. In portion 1, the flag, leaves and Canadian Healing Oil were used in the creation of a ritual space. In portion 2 there were the bringing of gifts and the cutting and clearing by the bands mother, equipped with a rod and appropriate gestures. In portion 3, notebooks and pencils were noticeable as symbolic objects of writing and gathering information, but it was through the sounds, the dancing, and singing that they communicated with each other and the ancestors. Portion 4, the revelation, was ich with symbols. The lantern, water, rhythm, dance and the dancer all played a part in giving meaning to the ritual. Portion 5 was a powerful display of rhythm, dance and colour. Portion 6 summed up the day's activity with the gift of croton leaves, the symbol of African spirituality, given to all who were privileged to enter the message room. The bands returned to their home churches feeling replenished to work the Watt Town message on their church seal. The croton leaves received at Watt Town by the leader of the bands was incorporated in the final ritual/ceremony at the church. It is at Watt Town that the iconography came together as a corpus representative of the core principles and religious systems of Revivalism.

CHAPTER 7

Iconography and Representation

The embodying of concepts, ideas and emotions in a symbolic form which can be transmitted and meaningfully interpreted is what we mean by the practices of representation.
—Stuart Hall[1]

In the preceding chapters, I looked at the sources that inform the Revival experience, the role of the iconography in the reconstruction of memory and the development of a symbolic system that creates and supports meaning. Understanding the importance of iconography to the philosophy and aesthetic core of the Revivalist movement, its role in cultural performances and the modes of identity it endorses, is important. It is the ideological pole it represents and the reality it presents that give meaning to the core concepts of Revivalism. It is important to note that while some of the concepts were influenced by the unconscious, much has been passed down from one generation to the next through the creation of strategic memory sites. These concepts have been preserved in the landscape, the seals, symbols, gestures, patterned movements and embodied technique.

The purpose of this chapter is to posit the view as to how the concepts put forward provided an African orientation for Revivalists/Revivalism and, by extension, African Jamaicans. My studies on diasporic religions, rituals, memory work and my research in Ghana allowed me to make some connections.

The Revival iconography is both prescriptive and performative. The prescriptive modes continue to reproduce the system while the performative mode is dynamic and allows for variation precisely because no two performances are alike. How the concepts portrayed by the iconography connect to Africa is important to an understanding of Revivalism. The performance of rituals and ceremonies provide the opportunity for these concepts to be made part and practice of the Revivalist experience.

"How easy it is to forget when there are no collective occasions for remembering," Lawrence Kirmayer once said.[2] Revivalists have ensured that all across the island there are collective occasions for the reconstruction of memory. The yearly visits to Watt Town could be described as homecoming for the Revivalists. The baptisms held at rivers and by the sea, especially on Sunday mornings at the different baptismal sites, the well-attended and sought after healing ceremonies, held sometimes twice per week in some churches, and the Revival tables that are popular among Revivalists as well as among a good cross-section of the Jamaican people all serve to keep the Afro-Jamaican memory alive among the practitioners and among those who sponsor tables as well as among the many onlookers. During these occasions, Revivalists come together and step away from their everyday activities to share time with each other and participate in songs, dances, rhythms and rituals that sustain their cultural values. The landscape's many features, including the seals, the signs, the foliage and the cemetery, are some of the tools used in the reconstruction of an ethnic community or distant homeland. The singing, dancing, rituals, colour, symbolism, dress and accessories all aid in the storing and transference of memory. The presence of the iconography in the churches and its use in rituals and ceremonies are strategic interventions to the hegemonic discourse. In this community, the people seek not only to honour the tradition of their ancestors but also to establish an identity that reflects the values and philosophy of generations of African Jamaican people.

The Revival network is made up of individuals who come together to form bands. This coming together allows for the pooling of information and the verification of that information among bands. There are many such bands established in different communities across the island. These bands come together at set periods at Watt Town and on other occasions like baptisms and tables. This process allows for the development of (1) a pool of information that satisfies the kind of corpus necessary for a tradition to represent the collective memory of a people, (2) a communication system through which Revivalists connect with each other across Jamaica, and (3) a system that creates and supports a body of knowledge that is culture-specific.

Memory Sites

All across the Jamaican landscape, African Jamaicans have created places of memory. These sites are important to African continuities in Jamaica. The perspective of the formerly enslaved is not found in textbooks but is preserved in these sites. In this chapter, through photographs taken in Ghana and Jamaica, and through the examination of Revival symbols that connect to Africa, I present some ways in which African Jamaicans recreate and preserve their African memories.

Last Bath

When I visited the ancestral park in Ghana, I was particularly struck by the similarities of the landscape at the site labelled the Last Bath to the baptism sites that can be found in different parts of Jamaica. Figure 66, a picture taken in Ghana, could be replicated at a number of baptism sites in Jamaica. Even more interesting was the vivid description given by the tour guide of how the enslaved Africans were cuffed, hands clasped, then dipped

FIGURE 66. Last Bath ancestral park in Ghana (2003)

face up in the water for their last bath before being put on the ship to the Caribbean. The clasping of the hands of the person to be baptized seemed representative of the slaves' hands being chained together when given their last bath. The baptized being dipped in the water face up is also a symbolic act reconnecting the baptized to their African heritage through water. The use of the term "newborn brother" takes on a special significance to African Jamaicans, as is demonstrated by the popularity of this water ritual among Revivalists and people from other churches.

To the people who travelled from all across the island to be baptized by Bedward and those who today are being baptized at different sites across the island, baptism is not only about accepting a Christian god but is an affirmation of their Africanness and the coming together of black people under the banner of an African Jamaican religion.

The all-nation flag (the red, gold and green flag in figure 23) planted at the baptism site signifies the African connection through water baptism. The establishing of the all-nation flag at the baptism site, Watt Town and in Revival churches is an act of reclamation of African heritage and a show of resistance against European dominance.

The Impini and Kindah Trees

During my visit to Acropong, a small town in Ghana, in November 2003, I went to the centre of the community to see the Impini tree. It is believed that the Jamaican village Accompong (located in St Elizabeth) is a replica of Acropong. In Acropong there is a housing complex that housed descendants of Jamaicans who returned to Ghana from Jamaica in the nineteenth century. I was particularly interested in this village because of Bishop Reid's claim that he is a descendant of the Maroons from Accompong.

The journey to Accompong reminded me of my journey to Acropong. The hills, the winding roads and the overall landscape were similar. The Impini tree is described by the people as a "reasoning tree". The community comes together to reason. It is under the Kindah tree in Accompong that the community sits and reasons.

FIGURE 67. Impini tree (also known as a "reasoning tree") in Acropong in Ghana (2003)

FIGURE 68. Kindah tree (also known as a "reasoning tree") in Accompong, Jamaica. (African Caribbean Institute of Jamaica)

Kumaci and Watt Town

"Thursday is the day of mourning when we remember our ancestors" – this was told to the visitors by a spokesman at Kumaci Palace (the Ashanti Kingdom) on 12 November 2003. The celebrations at Watt Town held on the first Thursday of every quarter seem to have a direct link to the Ashanti day of mourning. On the Thursday that I visited the palace in Kumaci, the king, who had just returned from London, was meeting with all the paramount chiefs in order to update them on his travels. He was welcomed with dance, song and speeches. There was a male dancer with an abeng who performed the role of a griot throughout the ceremony. Each paramount chief stood with a group of men under a large umbrella. There were only a few queen mothers among them. The other women sat on the seats in the building and watched the ceremony. All the people who attended the ceremony were dressed in black or a combination of black and maroon red. The umbrellas had bright colour combinations of maroon, gold, black, red, yellow, blue-black, gold and green-purple, orange, green and many other colours. The Asantehene

FIGURE 69. Wheel in the room of the second floor of the original building at Watt Town. It is placed in front of a window overlooking the sea (2003)

spoke in a language that was translated by a translator of the Twi language (Twi is the language retained by the Maroons).

As I watched the ceremony, I reflected on the Watt Town celebration and it occurred to me that the structure and purpose of both events had much in common. Each group led by a paramount chief could be compared to a Revival band led by a shepherd dressed in bright colour combinations. At Watt Town, all the Revival bands sit or stand in groups while one leader acts as master of ceremonies. The leader of each group that enters the church is given an opportunity to bring greetings and to share their stories with the gathering. The entire process – the trumping on the seals, the singing and dancing of the groups distinguished by colours, and, most of all, the very act of coming together as one people to pay homage to their ancestors – was an exercise in how a society remembers and reconstructs the past.

Watt Town acts as a symbolic anchor for a people who have had to refashion a religion and a culture that speaks to their needs. It also functions as a symbol of unity for the Revival people; the pilgrimage takes them back in time to those values and aesthetic principles from Africa, their ancestral homeland. The landscapes, plants, signs, sounds, smells and movements all play a significant role in the creation of a substitute homeland. All the elements

FIGURE 70. Drawing on the ground outside Elmino Castle, Ghana (2003)

FIGURE 71. Hut in a traditional village in Ghana (2003)

mentioned represent what Steven Feld and Keith Basso describe as the "multi-sensory conception of place".[3] These journeys remind the people of lost memories and bring them closer as an ancestral community. The rituals and ceremonies expressed play a critical role in how the group remembers and are therefore central to its collective memory. At Watt Town, the use of mnemonic devices come into play not only to celebrate and preserve the memories of Africa but also to foster cultural elements that endorse the structures and symbols that give Revivalism its legitimacy as an African Jamaican form.

FIGURE 72. Mother Nora's African hut, Westmoreland (2005). (Clinton Hutton)

Representation of African Gods

The drawings on the walls of the Sacred Heart Church and all the other churches are expressions of the people's belief system. The mermaid, the pool at the front of the church and the merman in the bishop's reading room speak to the importance of water spirits to the people who worship at Sacred Heart. The mix of signs represents the many spirit orders that the church embraces. The seals and symbols clearly connect to Africa. The iron pot and the chain are connected to the god of iron, Ogun. Margaret Thompson Drewal states that Ogun's symbolic complex consists of iron, the snake and the cutlass.[4] In figure 10, one can see a man's bust with two swords on the head, which is described by one of my informants as Michael, the protector who inspires much movement in the church and is represented by the colour red. The descriptions given of Michael are representative of the African god Shango, who is portrayed as the lord of the warriors, the spirit of battle.[5] He is also described as the great dancer who is celebrated by the colour red.[6] The symbols on the left side of the church in figures 9 and 10 resemble some of the symbols that represent the *loas* in Vodou. Courlander states that in Haitian Vodou, "Dambala is represented by a snake or the rainbow. Ogun is represented by the chains or iron bar, Shango/Michael the machete, the colour red, and the pot of fire."[7]

The hunter could be connected to the Akan god of the hunters, or it could be connected to Oshoosi (the brother of Ogun), who is the Yoruba god of the hunters.[8] The river mumma is connected to Yemoja of the Yoruba, the river god and sea god of the Ashante and other African water spirits. Yemoja is the same as Yemaja in the New World. Yemaja is referred to as the goddess of the ocean; she is represented in Jamaica by the ship's wheel and the mermaid. She is also associated with herbal medicine, and in her shrine are medicine vessels that resemble the "canopic jars" seen on Egyptian altars.[9] These jars bear a strong resemblance to the healing jars found in Revival churches in Jamaica (see figure 24). The water rituals (including the baptism ceremony), the pools and the basins are symbolic representations of the connectedness to African water spirits. The stone at the message seal at St Michael's and the movement motif in which one leg is represented as shorter than the other are connected to Esu or Legba, the African god of the crossroads.

Another symbol on the wall of Sacred Heart Church is the snake. Geoffrey Parrinder cites the snake as a symbol of rebirth, since it sheds its skin to go on living. The snake "with its tail in its mouth is an apt representation of an endless circle, a ring of eternity".[10] It is also represented in the Kongo, Dahomean and Fon retentions in the African diaspora: "Da or Dan, the good serpent of the skies, appears not only in Haiti but also in Cuba and in mixture with the Yoruba rainbow deity, Oshumare, in Brazil, that is wherever the Fon and their neighbors arrived as captives."[11]

The number seven is significant in Revivalism. All the altars I have seen have seven steps. The ritual readings of the Bible at tables include seven readings from the first to the seventh verse. Most of the churches studied have seven seals. The messenger seal in the church at Watt Town is made up of seven circles. Seven appears to be connected to the seven African gods. In three ceremonies of ordination of Revival bishops that I witnessed in three different parishes, seven Bibles were placed on the heads of the bishops being ordained. These seven Bibles could be a symbolic representation of some African gods, as well as the notion in African philosophy that "the human being is nothing until he learns to walk the seven directions".[12]

Signs from Ghana

Some of the signs on the buildings in Ghana in figure 73 are represented in Jamaican Revival churches. These signs are the Star of David, the snake, the

FIGURE 73. Old Fanti Village in Ghana, showing symbols that are also represented in Revival churches in Jamaica (2003)

flag, the chain, the two axes and the bird. They provide a link among the peoples of the African diaspora. All across the Atlantic these representations of African religion exist, and the iconography keeps what may have been an invisible culture visible.

Lineage Connection

The leaders of different churches maintain contact with different African spirits through the symbols and symbolic spaces. My research suggests that they keep in touch with their lineage through their special seal. In the churches mentioned in this study, one leader kept in touch with his Ashanti Maroon heritage through the river mumma pool, the merman and the Maroon pool (see figure 9). The merman could be connected to the Ashanti god Onyame, who is retained by the Maroons. "The major Ashanti gods are all male deities, the sons of Onyame the male high God – and they are all connected with water, the master symbol of fertility", states Turner.[13] Bishop Reid is a descendant of the Maroons; he gives fertility baths to women who are trying to have a child (see figure 15, which shows a merman and bath).

Another leader kept his Yoruba retentions through the hunter seal. This god/spirit has been Jamaicanized to carry a machete instead of a bow and arrow. Bishop Hill's church uses the number seven as his number and has on the main seal of the church twenty-one small flags on a metal ring. The symbolic representation of Oshoosi, the brother of Ogun, is more than a coincidence. "Oshoosi, the deity of hunters, is known by the iron bar on which is suspended seven or twenty-one pendants of Ogun", states Thompson.[14]

One church mother (Mother Yvonne Richards of Holt Close) is a fourth-generation healer who has also remained connected to her Bongo lineage through her association with the Bongo spirits. The bongo seal in her yard, her ability to play the bongo drums and the gifts of healing that she possesses (remnants or otherwise) all connect to her Bongo lineage.

Mother Nora's yard is a representation of a traditional African village (see figure 22). Its features include an African hut with African and African Jamaican symbols, the all-nation seal and pole, the benches and spaces for people to sit and talk to each other, a large kitchen, a fireplace, and rooms to accommodate the extended family.

Those who are at the top of the church hierarchy are those who not only boast of but can substantiate their strong African heritage. One of the ways to legitimize this heritage is the ability to manipulate the symbols to access spiritual powers. The fact that those who can best access African knowledge are placed high on the hierarchy makes Revivalism an institution that valorizes African retentions over any other.

Symbolic Movements and Behaviour

> Traditional dances give scope for conveying thought or matters of personal and/or social importance through the choice of signs and symbols, postures and facial expressionso.
> —E. Ampofo-Duodu[15]

There are a number of movements in Jamaican folk forms that could be traced back to Africa, but only a few will be highlighted in order to locate African philosophy within Revivalism. I catalogued some of the movements that are stable features of the Revival dance iconography and I now look at some of the messages these movements convey both in the African (Ghana) setting and in Revivalism.

One of the movement signs that I observed in the Sacred Heart Church is the placing of the index fingers together at the end of a movement phrase in which two people are involved. This motif is described earlier as a motif from the greeting ritual. The placing together of the two index fingers has been described by E. Ampofo-Duodu as the Ghanaian way of saying, "I am in love with you or we are one."[16] This sign is also cited by Gerald Jonas to mean "we are one people": "And the young man linked his two index fingers in front of him like two links in a chain, to indicate we are together, we cannot be separated, we are one people."[17] This symbol was seen at Kumaci, the Asantehene's palace in Ghana. In Jamaica it is represented in the Charles Town Maroon Museum and carries the same meaning: "we are together, we are one".

In this same setting at Kumaci, the U-shape form was observed. The chiefs, upon arrival at the palace, organized themselves into a U-shape formation to constitute a temporary court. The chief in charge of the ceremony sat at the base or closed end of the U, shaded by umbrellas held by attendants. The other people in the group were positioned on both sides of the U and they danced up and down the aisle, which is the space between the two sides of the U. This physical layout is similar to the setting at Sacred Heart Church and that seen at street meetings across the island. The basic movement used in this setting were "small steps that keep contact with the ground, shift their weight gracefully from hip to hip and move in a counterclockwise direction between the open end of the U and the closed end where the chief sits".[18] Opoku makes reference to a similar set of movements that character-ize Asante dance.[19] In the Revival iconography the "balance step" could be compared with the motif described by both Jonas and Opoku.

Other movement gestures that are similar and have shared meaning are the stomping of the feet, which means, "I will trample mine enemies." This gesture is used in Revivalism from the time of Bedward, who used it to trample his enemies. Another gesture cited by Ampofo-Duodu is "stretched arms with clenched fingers, which denotes power and strength".[20] This is used by Revival leaders in the same context.

The 60 Step

The 60 Step is the signature step of Revival dance. It appears to be closely related to an expression used by the Akan people. At a Jamaica Cultural Development Commission dance teachers' workshop on African retentions in the diaspora held in Kingston, Jamaica, in July 2004, Kariamu Welsh Asante, in looking at African retentions that have survived the New World, gave a demonstration of a combination in movement, rhythm and words, which is a sequence from the Akan people.

On the first stanza, a heavy step, called *ago* (which translates to "atten-tion"), is taken with the right foot with the torso inclined towards the earth. On the second stanza, another step, called *ame* (which translates to "I am listening"), is taken backwards with the right leg while the left hand is placed on the left ear and the left leg takes small steps close to the ground. She also explained that the stomping on the right leg is calling on the ancestors and the placing of the hand on the ears is saying, "We are listening for your response." This movement motif is similar to that of the 60 Step. The 60 Step is used when Revivalists circle and trump the seal in an anticlockwise direction in order to gain access to the spirit world. The climax of this exercise is possession by the spirits. This practice is also called "Myal" and is linked to the Maroon Akan tradition. The placing of the hand on the ear by a Revival leader when blowing the notes for the bands is representative of the Akan way of listening to the ancestors.

Myal or Ritual of the Circle

The ritual of the circle, or what is most commonly referred to as 60 or Myal, is the formation used for spirit work. The circle is the principal vehicle for African religion and is common to the people of both Central and West Africa. Moving anticlockwise around the seal is the high point of the Revival ceremony and is associated with ancestral ceremonies. It answers to the deepest spiritual need of African people and people of African descent because it speaks to ancestor communion. Once this ritual begins, the ceremony becomes totally African as the movement styles and the rhythms are reflective of the African aesthetics. Some of these principles are circularity, repetition, torso inclined forward, polyrhythm, and call-and-response. The constant use of these movements in the ceremony is directed to the ancestors and the spirits. Whenever spirit work is about to begin, the circle takes centre stage and all practitioners come together moving anticlockwise around the seal. The ritual of the circle functions as the visual sign of code-switching because it is at this juncture that the ceremony becomes African and, specifically, African Jamaican. This circle is also the symbol of unity between the many different African nations in Jamaica. When the practitioners enter the circle, all drumming ceases. It is the percussive movements of the body and the vocal sounds that provide the rhythms for this exercise. These rhythms are also symbolic of the coming together of the many drums of Africa.

Iconography, Meaning and Philosophy

It is the iconography that gives structure and meaning to the rituals of Revivalism. This is possible because the icons constitute a body of knowledge that is agreed upon by Revivalists. They agree upon a set of norms and practices even without being able to state why these are so. Hence they are not always able to logically explain the meanings that icons give to objects and ceremonies. These meanings are linked to their spiritual and historical experience. Experience is essential to meaning because meanings are tied to specific cultures and are shared by people who share the same culture.

At all the ceremonies mentioned in this text, the symbols served as vehicles for conveying meaning. In the healing ritual, the seven portions of the Watt Town ritual, the reading of the table or the Myal ritual circle, the iconography gave clarity and meaning to the ceremony. The ritual objects, drawings, colour, rhythm, songs, symbolic movements and patterns have allowed Revivalists to develop a system that creates and supports meaning.

The Revival way of life has captured the essence of African metaphysics, which is an understanding of the totality of one's reality. This includes all beings: God, ancestors, animals, plants and inorganic objects. Through iconography, rituals and ceremonies, Revivalists have given meaning to and interpreted their world through interactions among beings. The Revival philosophy, like African philosophy, is holistic and formed from the lived experience of Revival people.

P'Bitek, in his analysis of African philosophy, makes the point that men live in, belong to and work with institutions that are built around those things about which people are most concerned: their beliefs and ways of viewing the world. Hence philosophy is not only a set of ideas, and culture is not only a set of actions. Philosophy is the culture as lived and celebrated by the people. This supports the claim that African philosophy is not written and passed down in books but has instead been stored, practised and celebrated in folklore, folktales, folk art, religion, music and dance. These principles are in keeping with the notion that there are other ways of storing and retrieving knowledge than in scribal works and written research.

The seals, symbols and people articulate the Revival/Afro-Jamaican epistemology. The seals contain the text of Revivalism in the same way that the Bible contains the text of Christianity. This is the essence of Bishop Reid's analogy, "the Bible is to book as the seal is to the work". The iconography contains information that would be otherwise inaccessible. The song texts and the symbolic language are means of gaining knowledge on philosophical issues.

Although there are no records of African philosophical writings that have been handed down from one generation to another, all the branches that have been defined in philosophy – ontology, cosmology and aesthetics – can be discussed through the Revival iconography.

Ontology

The Jamaican Revivalist often speaks of power, its importance to spirit work and the importance of harnessing and protecting that power. The rituals and ceremonies in Revivalism are all directed at maintaining, accessing and manipulating that power. The relationship among beings is essential in Revivalism. The link between God, the spirits, ancestors, man, animals, vegetable and organic forces forms the ontological system that preserves and gives sustenance to the Revival world view.

In the Bantu ontology, the term "being" is interchangeable with "force". "All beings in the universe possess vital forces – force is Being, being is force", states Placide Tempels in his essay "Bantu Philosophy".[21] Tempels also posits that all beings possess vital force that can strengthen or weaken the vital energy of man. Men pray to God and the spirits to maintain this energy because it is believed that suffering and illness come when this force is weakened or lost. This same concept was expressed in his discussion of the Ifa ontological background: "Ashe, often translated as 'power' is a concept that designates the dynamism of being and the very vitality of life."[22]

The Revival iconography not only confirms the presence of these forces but assists in creating liminal spaces that facilitate interaction among beings. In analysing portion 1 of Watt Town, the ontological journey, the importance of the interaction of different beings in order to create the magic or power necessary for the success of the ritual is clear. In this suite, flags, plants, oils and the inclusion of the spirit force through the symbolic circle formed by human bodies, give a picture of the total reality of being. "Ashe", in other words, is the "force of coherence of process itself, that which makes a system a system".[23] All across the Revival landscape and the black diaspora, black people have found ways of recreating and reconstructing African religion and world view with the aid of mnemonic devices mobilized by force. This reconstruction is also a reconstruction of self, an identity project. During possession dancing, the body is an icon that both experiences and showcases the dance of the ancestors; hence the act of losing oneself is essentially the act of reclaiming one's ancestry. The seals at Watt Town and other sites provide a space for the relationship or interaction of forces.

The movement motifs of cutting and clearing and "tun yu roll" are Revival philosophy in motion. All across the island these movements are meant to dismiss evil. This theory of binding and loosing is at the heart of Vodou philosophy. Brown writes: "In order to get things flowing among persons and between spirits, gates have to be opened, pathways cleared, chains broken, blockages removed and knots untied."[24] Richards suggests that it is this kind of philosophy that remains the indomitable strength of a people plagued by political powerlessness.[25] The Revival philosophy of cutting and clearing remains functional for hundreds of African Jamaicans who believe that they will be overcome by sickness, suffering and problems when their power (force) is weakened or lost.

This power is important to those who aspire to lead, whether as a Revival leader or an African chief. "A chief who is not able by reason of his vital rank or vital force, to be the link binding dead and living, such a one cannot be chief. It is impossible", Tempels states.[26] The leadership crisis experienced by Bishop Reid and his church community after an illness that left him paralysed was due to the fact that he no longer had the power to mobilize the forces. He was no longer able to dance and experience his religion to the fullest.

Working the seals at Watt Town is important to the acquisition of power. The revival leaders work the physician seal at Watt Town in order to interact with the messengers. It is through this exercise they are able to make contact with the spirit world and in so doing they are empowered.

The journey to Watt Town is ontological because it binds people together and binds them to their creator as well. It is this exposure to the ontological system that sustains the Revival world view. The sharing in song and movement and the bringing of material gifts to the shrine in order to receive spiritual gifts like the croton leaves and spiritual communion from the many seals are an affirmation of the Revivalist way of seeing the world and the ontological underpinnings of ways of being.

The hosting of Revival tables is very important to the principle of the Revival ontology of honouring the customs of ancestors. Mother Nora and

Leader Wollery had to come back from England and Mother Millie had to come back from the United States in order to put on their annual thanksgiving table to honour the tradition. They all felt they would have died if they did not come back to Jamaica to put on these tables. Tempels supports this in the following observation made in 1936: "I gave my normal class students at Lukonzolwa (Lake Moero) as an essay subject, 'Obstacles to conversion among pagan people. To my astonishment, so far from setting out a list of practices, all of them declared that the great obstacle could be summed up in a conviction that to abandon the customs appointed by the ancestors would lead to death."[27] This view is as common among Revivalists as it is among Africans. It is also the only logical explanation for the popularity of the hosting of these elaborate and expensive tables by Revivalists across Jamaica.

Cosmology and Iconography

The Revival iconography has been used by Revival practitioners to order their religion and bring a visible and practical dimension to their belief system. Iconography helps to order the world of the Revivalists and hold the system of interdependent parts together as a whole.

An analysis of the Revival iconography gives a clear picture of how the cosmology is experienced by the practitioners. The physical design of the church and all its icons and symbols facilitate the ordering and interpretation of the Revival cosmology. The altar satisfies the duality of the religion. It represents Christianity and God ("Massa God"), who is placed above all other forces but maintains a distance in everyday activities. In one of the churches visited, the woman who looks after the altar is deemed as sacred. She is someone who has passed menopause and is no longer sexually active. "This is to ensure that she is always clean." Spirit work does not take place in this area. The functions of the altar were described by two bishops as decorative, and the use of the space in other churches confirms this notion. The icons in this area are the Bible and a picture of the the Last Supper, figures of angels and the Virgin Mary. The altar is also the area where the hierarchy of the church sits during testimony, Bible reading and the singing of hymns.

The many seals on Revival sites facilitate spirit work and ensure the flow of ancestral wisdom. In all the rituals and ceremonies, whether it be healing, tables, transfer of leadership, empowerment of leaders and members or any kind of activity described by members as spirit work, the seals are central to these activities. The large space in the middle of the church facilitates the movement and dancing necessary for spirit work. There is plenty of space for the bands to circle the seals during the different rituals and ceremonies. Bishop Reid's comment that "Seal crown all, Bible to Book, Seal to crown the work" must be underscored. It is within these liminal spaces that participants can best experience their religion as they are empowered to cross the threshold from the human to the spirit world.

The presence of the croton on all sites, its use in welcoming and greeting the spirits, and the gift of a branch of croton to all the practitioners who attend the ceremony at Watt Town all endorse the African presence in Revivalism.

The practitioners' dress and accessories carry many messages about the culture. See, for example, figure 56, which shows a woman carrying the Bible and croton. This picture is the visual representation of two religions sharing the same space: Christianity and African religion. To her and other Revivalists, this is not problematic because Revival cosmology is ordered to facilitate the sharing. The young leader in figure 55, holding his pencil and notebook in readiness to record the messages and whispers from the ancestors, signifies that there are other ways of knowing. The marking of the seal speaks to the preparation that invites and ensures the involvement of the spirit force. The tomb in figure 5, furnished with food, drink and other gifts, and the Revival tables are symbols of the offerings of libation and the veneration of ancestors. The carrying of gifts to Watt Town in figure 50 also keeps in memory the African value of reciprocity: one gives in order to receive. The practitioners bring their gifts in order to receive spiritual guidance and fulfilment. The Watt Town leader in figure 61 collecting the messages from the groves of crotons in order to prepare them for the bands (figure 62) and distribute them to all the practitioners as they trump anticlockwise around the seal is the final ritual activity for the day. This sharing of croton leaves, the symbol of African spirituality, is an act of ancestor communion. The bands returning to their home churches all across Jamaica with their spiritual gifts (figure 64) personify for the participants their experience of African religion.

The cosmology is ordered and given a practical dimension through the iconography. The organization of the space and the icons facilitates the sharing of the space by both Christianity and African religion. Where the church is situated on the continuum can be determined by the visibility of the icons and how they are used. Different symbols take centre stage for the enactment of specific rituals, and different rituals or stages of a ritual take place in specific spaces.

The symbols, spaces, objects and plants represent a cosmology that is holistic in principle and function. They also make it possible for the practitioners to gain access to the spiritual world and thereby experience their religion to the fullest. "Cosmology comes to incorporate the experiential world of ordinary people so that ways of understanding and dealing with it take centre stage", writes Michael Herzfeld.[28] Revival practitioners have used the deployment of iconography to bring a practical dimension to the Revival cosmology, one that is reflective of an African cosmology in which all life experiences can be made part of the practitioners' religious experiences.

Performance and Aesthetics

It is in the area of performance that the Revivalist best engages life. The performance spaces in Revivalism, the liminal spaces and the seals are the spaces in which the oppressed are able to dance the dance of history and reclaim their humanity. Through these transformed spaces and practices, they release themselves from being the colonized object or thing without a history or a culture. These performances are self-redeeming. Ironically, it is the struggle that motivates the engagement of the indigenous culture. Judith Hanna, on the subject of aesthetic value, refers to notions of appropriateness, form, content, style, qualities and features.[29] In chapter 5, I discussed the singing, the content of the songs, the dance, rhythmic exercise, ritual and drama – all of which form part of the aesthetic core of Revivalism. It is the cultural performances that reveal the aesthetic preferences of the people. These performances also affirm what is important to them and what is appropriate for each occasion. It is evident that the characteristics of African aesthetics – holism, repetition, improvisation, circularity, epic memory and the paradigm of rhythmic text – are also central to Revival culture. This is the nature of Revivalism: the music, the dance, colour and symbolism. Holism is that element that sustains the Revival world view and it is the iconography that pulls all these elements together into a unified whole.

Repetition is an important feature of Revivalism. The annual events like thanksgiving tables and the quarterly presentation of events like Watt Town allow for events to be repeated at set periods. Repetition, whether of a single event or the elements within rituals, have the potential to unify people, provide a continuous reference to the collective pool of information and give stability and structure to rituals and cultural forms. The cues in movement, rhythm, song and colour can be recalled and repeated. The constant repetition of the elements serves to intensify the statements being made and to clarify communication. Repetition of rhythm and chorus is one of the aesthetic qualities in Revivalism that is also part of the aesthetic core of African Jamaican music and dance. The iconography not only helps to provide the constants that can be repeated but also gives the cues that differentiate the frames of the ritual.

The call-and-response feature ensures participation, collective response and affirmation. During the sermon, the leader seeks the approval or opinion of the flock through this practice. In Jamaica we may not sing the same songs or speak the same language as our ancestors did in Africa, but the Jamaican people have found ways to recreate and transform African beliefs and practices to meet the demands of their new environment through forms such as Revivalism. These structures facilitate the communication of coded messages in communities that for the most part have transmitted their traditions orally.

Another important feature of African aesthetics that has been maintained in Revivalism is improvisation. Improvisation is the art of manoeuvring embodied techniques and is important to the processual understanding of rituals. It allows for variation and the introduction of new text within the rituals. Hence a Revival ritual performed one night will be different on another night at the same place. Although the elements will be the same and the people will be the same, the ritual will not be identical. This is one of the qualities of Revivalism that allows for the fluidity and flexibility necessary to allow for the inclusion of practices of everyday life.

These characteristics of African traditions that have been maintained in Revivalism have given the religion the capacity to rejuvenate itself in changing circumstances and continue to survive. As Ni Yarte puts it, "When you understand the rules of a tradition you can move forward and the society will accept it."[30]

Rhythmic Text

Music and dance make up the paradigm of rhythmic text. It is an essential feature in African and Revival aesthetics. It provides both structure and energy for the ritual ceremonies, such as the healing ceremony. The songs and music have to be appropriate in order to access spiritual powers; it is the movement and music that best identify the different frames of the rituals. The blowing of notes and the dance make it possible for the union of man and spirits. Meaning is linked to these rhythms and they form the text for the iconography of sound. Exercises such as the drilling of the bands and blowing the notes for the bands are techniques developed in Revivalism; these techniques demonstrate how the rhythmic structure of different African languages and their magical powers have been passed on from one generation to the next.

Through body stance and posturing – such as the torso inclined forward, groundedness, circularity and possession dancing – the movement that forms the core of the Revival dance iconography is constantly expressed. The Revival aesthetics, like the African aesthetics, are functional, organic and relevant to the lives of Revival people. The aesthetic principles inform and support the Revival culture.

Ritual Performance and Iconography

It is the iconography that pulls the ritual performances together in Revivalism. The visuals, the smells, the sound, the colour, the music and dance come together for the overall performance. These performances can be with man or with the spirit through the possession of an individual in a solo performance or a number of people in a group performance. Victor Turner and Edith Turner describe these performances as a "complex sequence of symbolic acts".[31] Whether the performances are at a baptism, healing ritual or table, the icons used play a critical role in the fulfilment of the ritual. These symbolic acts represent all the modes of non-verbal communication and are ways in which cultural themes, values and beliefs are communicated and reinforced. Symbols and gestures play an important role in the transition from one phase of the ritual to the next. They signify what is happening at each stage of the ritual, and they ratify and make visual the intent of the ceremony.

These icons and functions have been passed down through generations. The landscape has been made a part of the rituals while the music and dance sustain the energy, but it is the many performances of the rituals and ceremonies that ultimately maintain the traditions and make them relevant to contemporary life. The iconography plays an important role in giving meaning and clarity to these cultural performances. It also provides the magic that inspires a sense of awe and gives the rituals an air of invincibility. It is at Watt Town and in the rituals of baptism, healing ceremonies and the tables that the iconography comes together and allows the people to affirm the validity of these icons, whether in the visual, auditory or kinetic sense.

Even if there are variations in the icons and symbols used in different churches and variations in the ways they are used, it is evident that different bands from across the island work together and understand each other. The Revival iconography is established and widely known across the island. The working of the seals and colour codes and the use of icons like the flags, crotons and water in the rituals and ceremonies are understood by Revivalists and a large number of African Jamaicans who attend or watch the ceremonies.

Revivalism is the performance of an identity. Through a variety of iconic forms, Revivalists have developed a kind of language or "culture grammar" that practitioners and, by extension, African Jamaicans can use to communicate in an African way. This language, expressed through different performance modes, is an embodiment of the people's belief and is representative of how they see themselves. The coming together of the many African rhythms through the blowing of notes, doing spirit work in the Myal circle, moving anticlockwise around the seal and the planting of the all-nation flag on Revival sites are all expressions of African reality among Revivalists.

The philosophy is thus encoded in the iconography – the seals, the symbols, the music and dance are imbued with meaning and the practitioners understand and can interpret these meanings. Joseph Omoregbe made the point that philosophy is reflective of human experiences and that these reflections and views can be preserved and transmitted through channels other than writing, through what he calls, "objects of knowledge".[32]

Conclusion

Revivalism, the first Jamaican religion, is also praxis as manifested in the extensive rituals and ceremonies that characterize it as a Jamaican cultural phenomenon.

Counterhegemonic forms, like Revivalism, responded to the historical and social conditions of plantation society and the dominant ideologies of the ruling class that were oppressive to the people's African ethos. Its emergence can be described not only as a cultural form but as a source of cultural power. Revivalists have taken objects such as flags, candles, water and colour codes, including the colours red, white and blue – all symbols of the dominant (European) group – and they have re-appropriated these symbols and meanings to signify their "Africanness", while at the same time resisting the ideologies of the master class.

As Stuart Hall states: "What matters most are not the intrinsic or histori-cally fixed objects of culture but the state of play in cultural relations."[33] This frame of thinking has been translated into African lenses, and the meaning of objects and symbols is organized and translated through iconographic codes. These codes serve as maps of meaning to a people in the process of becoming. The Revival space has become a space where people of African descent have been successful in framing and preserving an ideology of blackness. The extent to which these ideologies have influenced the wider society is not the focus of this book, but these ideologies have certainly influenced the wider society, especially the spaces of the poor and working class. The music and dance of Revivalism, which originate from Jamaica, make a statement as to how African codes of meaning have influenced the aesthetic preferences of the Afro-Jamaican people.

Revivalism has established a most expansive network for the development of Afro-Jamaican philosophy: ontology, cosmology and aesthetics. The corpus has been a base from which a collective response to that which is important to the majority of Afro-Jamaicans has always found release. Many things that are sanctioned by the collective will of the people have been made part of the Revival experience. People give meaning and significance to objects based on their own understanding of the cultural order.

Through the establishment and functions of seals and symbols in the different ceremonies, culture is historically reproduced. The Watt Town experience is an enactment of African cultural patterns, hence young leaders go to be immersed in the traditions. This is not to say that things are done at Watt Town or in Revival churches across the island precisely as they are done in Africa but that the events are organized in terms of an African past. Representation is not about absolute truth or fixed meanings but about a discourse that creates the space for the production of meaning.

Because the Revival iconography is both prescriptive and performative, we are assured that the dialogue with history will continue and even in the face of change the present will remain true to the past. It is the iconography that has kept and preserved the spirituality, ideology and aesthetic modes of Afro-Jamaican people. The liminal spaces created by the iconography have allowed for the inclusion of alternative voices. It is also within these spaces that practitioners have been empowered through spiritual healing, rhythm and dance to perform rituals that are reflective of their African identity and to obtain spiritual guidance for their families and their communities. Stuart Hall makes the point that "meaning is what gives us a sense of our own identity, of who we are and with whom we belong – so it is tied up with questions of how culture is used to mark out and maintain identity within and difference between groups".[34]

It is through these cultural performances and the meaning they produce that Revivalists reaffirm and reconstruct their African identity and redeem their humanity. By affirming these practices, African Jamaicans have also been able to resist oppressive ideologies. The Revival iconography reflects and articulates African patterns and sensibilities and serves as a positive agent in maintaining these patterns and ideologies for both practitioners and onlookers.

Revivalism presents a counternarrative to colonialism through symbolic language. Colonialism seeks to control a people's politics and wealth and, most importantly, their culture – how they value and see themselves. Colonialists took away a people's language in order to alienate them from their history and their culture. "To speak a language is to take on a culture and to assume a culture is to support the weight of a civilization", says Frantz Fanon.[35] The Revival iconography provided the language that allowed Revivalists to reconnect with African metaphysics and reclaim their African self. It is the key that opens metaphysical spaces, the key that releases the sound images locked in past memories. Bishop Bourne likens it to a key to a vault and Pastor Queenie calls it a key or a note to which she must respond.

The Revival iconography is a language that reflects the people's experience, documents their culture and brings clarity to social and religious processes. This language embodies identity and community. It is able to do this through many modes because it is multisensory and extends beyond words, through the visual, smell, touch and kinetic sensibility. It carries the particularity of the sounds, images, smells and movement of the world it represents, a world that is "really real" to Revivalists. As Geertz puts it:

> it is this sense of the "really real" upon which the religious perspective rests and which the symbolic activities of religion as a cultural system are devoted to producing, intensifying, and, so far as possible, rendering inviolable by the discordant revelations of secular experience. It is, again, the imbuing of a specific complex of symbols – of the metaphysic they formulate and the style of life they recommend – with a persuasive authority which, from an analytic point of view, is the essence of religious action.[36]

The dance, rituals and other performance styles serve as vehicles of continuity with Africa. It is through performance that the iconography becomes a practical whole in the system of meaning. It is the symbols that motivate meaning and create the mood for metaphysical concepts through which Revivalists represent themselves and their belief system in the performance of a world that, to them, is "really real".

What is "really real" to Revivalists is the contact with ancestors and African metaphysics. Through inscribing and incorporating practices (embodied experience), they create a vision of Africa. The performance practices, rituals, song and dance bring all these icons together to make the view real. Through the use of iconography, they create liminal spaces to act out their philosophy. People who are hedged in draw on their symbolic capacities to open up more space for them to practise their religion. Through the deployment of iconography and performance, Revivalists are able to open up a larger world for themselves. This larger world is their vision of Africa.

By virtue of the Christian elements in Revivalism, it cannot be considered just an African religion, but it is the connection with Africa that is most important to the people. It is their interpretation of these African continuities that engages their being as to who they really are. Fragmented or otherwise, the rituals of Revivalism have served to challenge foundation histories and to create openings for narratives of the past to inform the present.

All across the island, Revival leaders are holding bands together with practices such as drilling the bands, blowing the notes, singing, dancing and ritual activity. They are, as Brandon states, "incorporating cultural memory into habitual patterns of social interaction, movement and body postures, as well as materializing abstract religious concepts in creating icons, or other acts of transfer and memory keeping".[37]

Through these practices, ceremonies, music and dance the collective ethos has found expression. The performance and repetition of these activities have laid the foundation for the development of African Jamaican aesthetics. Music and dance techniques have been used for decades by Revivalists to gain access to wisdom, healing and a sense of self through "ancestorism" or "epic memory". Revivalism embodies the belief system of the people. It pulls together a number of performative elements that include gestures, dress, headdress and the use of symbols as a representation of self and an African Jamaican identity. Although the seals and symbols of different Revival leaders may not always look the same, they provide common grounds for the affirmation of a collective identity.

It is the Revival iconography that sets Revivalism apart from all other religions and cultural forms and gives it its legitimacy as an African-Jamaican phenomenon. The seals and symbols, the iconic spaces, rituals and ceremonies, colour codes, dress, accessories, music, and dance are all part of a body of knowledge that guards the African legacy, echoes the people's world view and provides the signifiers for the performance of an African Jamaican identity.

Glossary

all-nation. The coming together of peoples from all the nations of Africa under one umbrella. This could be compared with pan-Africanism.

bands. Each Revival group/church is called a bands.

blow the notes. Rhythmic sounds made by the leader to assist communication with the spirits.

croton. The scientific name of this plant is *Codieaum variegatum*. Many varieties are found across the island, especially on Revival sites and burial sites. It has been described as the representation of African spirituality in Jamaica.

cut and clear. This term means to clear away evil with a chopping movement of the hands (for example, to move evil spirits and bad luck) from one's surroundings.

journey. Travelling on a spiritual journey; to be possessed by a spirit, which sends you on a spiritual journey.

Maypole. A traditional dance done around a pole. Ribbons of different colours are wrapped around the pole, making different patterns.

members meaning. The meaning as shared with me by Revival members, and the names that they use to describe the ritual and ceremonies.

messengers. Spirits who come to participate in the ceremonies.

Myal. Myal was the religion practised by the Maroons, who are descendants of the Ashanti Koromanti people. Possession is the essence of this religion, hence to "come under Myal" is to be possessed. Myalism is also the forerunner to Revivalism. (See chapter 2 for more information.)

order. Ceremonies of the church; how the ceremony is structured and the elements included in the ceremony.

possession. During possession, the human body is temporarily inhabited by spirits.

reader. Forecaster of the future.

releasing the spirit. A tradition among some Revivalists and Kumina people of releasing the spirit of the dead before burial so that the spirit might be free to return to Africa. This tradition is found among some Revivalists as well as Kumina devotees.

seal. Seals are sacred spaces; they are the most important areas of the church. All important rituals are performed on a seal. (See chapter 4 for details.)

symbol. Objects used in Revival ceremonies which are endowed with special meaning, for example, flags, water. (See chapter 4 for details.)

60. A brand of Revivalism that demonstrates more Christian elements than African. It is sometimes called "original Zion" and is associated with the Great Revival of 1860 among the ex-slaves. The number 60 is marked on the seals and symbols.

61. A brand of Revivalism that demonstrates more African elements than Christian.

60 Step. This movement motif is a signature step in Revivalism. It is mostly used around the seal when the bands circle the seal for spirit work. It is sometimes described as "trumping".

sign in. To register one's presence on the seal to do spirit work. This could be compared with registration in a Western setting, e.g. registering for a conference.

spirit work. A ritual process through which devotees make contact and commune with the spirit force.

trumping. Heavy steps to a rhythm; usually done on or around a seal.

tun you roll. To turn in different directions to be set free from evil spirits.

unseen guests. This usually refers to spirits.

Notes

Chapter 1

1. Barry Chevannes, *Rastafari and other African-Caribbean Worldviews* (1995; repr., New Brunswick, NJ: Rutgers University Press, 1998), 22–23.

2. Thomas F. Heck, *Picturing Performance: The Iconography of the Performing Arts in Concept and Practice* (Rochester, NY: University of Rochester Press, 1999), 19.

3. Chevannes, *Rastafari*, 6.

4. Walter Pitts, *Old Ship of Zion: The Afro-Baptist Ritual in the African Diaspora* (Oxford: Oxford University Press, 1993), 98.

5. Edward Seaga, "Revival Cults in Jamaica: Notes towards a Sociology of Religion", *Jamaica Journal* 3, no. 2 (1969): 13.

6. Melville J. Herskovits, *The Myth of the Negro Past* (Boston: Beacon Press, 1958), 81.

7. Clifford Geertz, *The Interpretation of Cultures: Selected Essays* (New York: Basic Books, 1973), 112.

8. Jan Vansina, *Oral Tradition as History* (Madison: University of Wisconsin Press, 1985), 148.

9. Okot P'Bitek, "The Sociality of Self", in *African Philosophy: An Anthology*, ed. E.C. Eze (Malden, MA: Blackwell, 2001), 73.

10. Victor Turner, *The Ritual Process: Structure and Anti-structure* (Hawthorne, NY: Aldine De Gruyter, 1969), 95.

11. Paul Stoller, *Embodying Colonial Memories: Spirit Possession, Power and the Hauka in West Africa* (New York: Routledge, 1995), 29–35.

12. Stuart Hall, *Representation: Cultural Representations and Signifying Practices* (London: Sage, 1997), 5.

Chapter 2

1. Robert J.C. Young, *Colonial Desire: Hybridity in Theory, Culture and Race* (London: Routledge, 1995), 51.

2. Barry Chevannes, *Rastafari: Roots and Ideology* (Syracuse: Syracuse University Press, 1995), ix.

3.   Rex Nettleford, *Inward Stretch, Outward Reach* (London: Macmillan, 1993), 84; Chevannes, *Rastafari*, 17.

4.   Bishop Reid, personal communication with the author, March 1978.

5.   Rex Nettleford, "The Caribbean Creative Diversity: The Defining Point of the Region's History" (paper presented at Dancing across Disciplines, Intercultural Dance and Music Institute, Miami, Florida, 2000), 12.

6.   Hope Waddell, *Twenty-Nine Years in the West Indies and Central Africa: A Review of Missionary Work and Adventure, 1829–1858* (London: Nelson, 1970), 197.

7.   Joseph J. Williams, *Jamaican Witchcraft* (Westport, CT: Greenwood, 1934), 70.

8.   Edward Long, *History of Jamaica*, volume 2: *Reflections on Its Situation, Settlements, Inhabitants, Climate, Products, Commerce, Laws, and Government* (London: Lowndes, 1974), 451–52.

9.   Orlando Patterson, *The Sociology of Slavery: An Analysis of the Origins, Development and Structure of Negro Slave Society in Jamaica* (London: Granada, 1973), 276.

10.   Irvin Markovitz, *Power and Class in Africa* (Englewood Cliffs, NJ: Prentice Hall, 1977), 111.

11.   Barbara Kopytoff, "The Development of Jamaican Maroon Ethnicity", *Caribbean Quarterly* 22, nos. 2–3, (1976): 42.

12.   Williams, *Jamaican Witchcraft*, 67.

13.   Kenneth Bilby, "Black Thoughts from the Caribbean", *New West Indian Guide* 57, nos. 3–4 (1983): 201–14.

14.   Monica Schuler, "Myalism and the African Religious Tradition in Jamaica", in *Africa and the Caribbean: The Legacies of the Link*, ed. M. Crahan and F.W. Knight (Baltimore: Johns Hopkins University Press, 1979), 173.

15.   A.M. Opoku, "Asante Dance Art and the Court", in *The Golden Stool: Studies of the Asante Center and Periphery*, ed. Enid Schildkrout, Anthropological Papers of the American Museum of Natural History, vol. 65, part 1 (New York: American Museum of Natural History, 1987), 192–99.

16.   John Mbiti, *African Religions and Philosophy* (New York: Doubleday, 1969), 112.

17.   Waddell, *Twenty-Nine Years*, 189.

18.   *Parliamentary Papers*, 1866: 3.

19.   Ibid., 15.

20.   Ibid., 46.

21.   Ibid., 55.

22.   Louis Marriott, *Bedward* (play), 8.

23.   http://archives.jard.gov.jm/index.php/marcus-garvey-said-up-you-mighty-race-you-can-accomplish-what-you-will-quotations-collected-by-ken-jones.

24. Chevannes, *Rastafari*, 39.
25. Mervyn Alleyne, *Roots of Jamaican Culture* (London: Pluto, 1988), 101.
26. Seaga, "Revival Cults", 13.
27. Herskovits, *Myth of the Negro Past*, 50.
28. Noel Leo Erskine, *Decolonizing Theology: A Caribbean Perspective* (Maryknoll, NY: Orbis, 1981), 142.
29. Nettleford, *Inward Stretch*, 80.
30. Chevannes, *Rastafari*, 22.
31. Robert J. Stewart, *Religion and Society in Post-Emancipation Jamaica* (Knoxville: University of Tennessee Press, 1992), 135–36.

Chapter 3

1. Seaga, "Revival Cults".
2. Ibid., 8.
3. Unless otherwise indicated, all quotes from church leaders and members are taken from the interviews and personal communication with the author during fieldwork. A comprehensive list appears at the end of the bibliography.
4. Harold Courlander, *The Drum and the Hoe: Life and Lore of the Haitian People* (Berkeley: University of California Press, 1960), 14.
5. Ibid., 15.
6. Hall, *Representation*, 5.

Chapter 4

1. Barbaro Martínez-Ruiz, "Mambo Comes from the Soul", in *Call and Response: Journeys in African Art*, ed. Sarah Adams, Barbaro Martínez-Ruiz, Robert Farris Thompson, Joanna Weber and Lyneise Williams (New Haven, CT: Yale University Gallery Press, 2000), 94.
2. Robert Farris Thompson, *Flash of the Spirit: African and Afro-American Art and Philosophy* (New York: Random House, 1983), 108.
3. Paul Connerton, *How Societies Remember* (Cambridge: Cambridge University Press, 1989), 14.
4. Geertz, *Interpretation*, 129.
5. Ibid., 93.
6. Dominique Zahan, "Some Reflections on African Spirituality", in *African Spirituality: Forms, Meanings and Expressions*, ed. Jacob K. Olupona (New York: Crossroad, 2000), 15.

7.   Ibid.
8.   Ibid.
9.   Victor Turner, *The Forest of Symbols: Aspects of Ndembu Ritual* (Ithaca: Cornell University Press, 1967), 30–32.
10.   Thompson, *Flash*, 172.
11.   George Eaton Simpson, *Religious Cults of the Caribbean: Trinidad, Jamaica, and Haiti* (Puerto Rico: Institute of Caribbean Studies, University of Puerto Rico, 1970), 82–83.
12.   Ibid.
13.   Ibid.
14.   Ni Yarte, in conversation at the conference "The Dance of Our Ancestors", Temple University, Philadelphia, 12 January 2005.

Chapter 5

1.   Stewart, *Religion and Society*, 134.
2.   Turner, *Ritual Process*, 167.
3.   Dona Richards, "The Implications of African American Spirituality", in *African Culture*, ed. M.K. Asante and K.W. Asante (Trenton, NJ: Africa World Press, 1990), 224.
4.   Bruce Mannheim, "Iconicity", in *Key Terms in Language and Culture*, ed. Alessandro Duranti (Oxford: Blackwell, 2001), 103.
5.   Connerton, *How Societies Remember*, 76.
6.   Edward Seaga, "River Maid, River Maid", *Jamaica Journal* 3, no. 2 (1969): 17.
7.   Richards, "Implications", 14.
8.   Patrick Taylor, *Nation Dance: Religion, Identity and Cultural Difference in the Caribbean* (Kingston: Ian Randle, 2001), 2.
9.   Barbara Browning, *Samba: Resistance in Motion* (Bloomington: Indiana University Press, 1995), 35.
10.   Victor Turner, *The Anthropology of Performance* (New York: PAJ Publications, 1988), 166.
11.   George Brandon, *Santeria from Africa to the New World: The Dead Sell Memories* (Bloomington: Indiana University Press, 1997), 140.
12.   Inger Sjørslev, "Possession and Syncretism: Spirits as Mediators in Modernity", in *Reinventing Religions: Syncretism and Transformation in Africa and the Americas*, ed. André Droogers and Sidney M. Greenfield (New York: Rowman and Littlefield, 2001), 136.
13.   Linda Giles, "Spirit Possession and the Symbolic Construction of Swahili

Society", in *Spirit Possession: Modernity and Power in Africa*, ed. Heike Behrend and Ute Luig (Madison: University of Wisconsin Press, 1999), 143.

14. Esther Dagan, *The Spirit's Dance in Africa: Evolution, Transformation, and Continuity in Sub-Sahara* (Westmount, QC: Galerie Amrad African Arts Publications, 1997), 122.

15. Barry Chevannes, "Revival and Black Struggle", *Savacou* 5 (1971): 31.

Chapter 6

1. Jacob Climo, and Maria Cattel, eds., *Social Memory and History: Anthropological Perspectives* (New York: AltaMira Press, 2002), 35.

2. Turner, *Ritual Process*, 6.

3. Richards, "Implications", 212.

4. Simpson, *Religious Cults*, 184.

5. Karen McCarthy Brown, "Systematic Remembering, Systematic Forgetting: Ogou in Haiti", in *Africa's Ogun: Old World and New*, ed. Sandra T. Barnes (Bloomington: Indiana University Press, 1997), 214.

6. Richards, "Implications", 213.

7. Barry Chevannes, lecture on Caribbean culture at the University of the West Indies, Mona, Jamaica, 2003.

8. Jamake Highwater, *Dance: Rituals of Experience* (Oxford: Oxford University Press, 1978), 14.

9. Frances J. Crosby, "He Hideth My Soul" (1860).

Chapter 7

1. Hall, *Representation*, 10.

2. Lawrence Kirmayer, quoted in Climo and Cattell, *Social Memory*, 3.

3. Steven Feld and Keith H. Basso, eds., *Senses of Place* (Santa Fe, NM: School of American Research Press, 1996), 97.

4. Margaret Thompson Drewal, *Yoruba Ritual: Performers, Play, Agency* (Bloomington: Indiana University Press, 1992), 261.

5. Thompson, *Flash*, 90.

6. Fra Ananael 138 and Sor. OchO/148, "The Seven African Gods" (manuscript, n.d.), 10.

7. Courlander, *Drum*, 8.

8. Thompson Drewal, *Yoruba Ritual*, 57.

9. Fra Ananael and Sor. OchO, "Seven African Gods", 15.

10. Geoffrey Parrinder, *Encountering World Religions: Questions of Religious Truth* (Edinburgh: T. and T. Clark, 1987), 128.
11. Thompson, *Flash*, 176.
12. Kimbwandende Kia Fu-Kiau Bunseki, *Tying the Spiritual Knot: African Cosmology of the Bântu-Kôngo: Principles of Life and Living* (Brooklyn: Athelia Henrietta Press, 2001), 135.
13. Turner, *Ritual Process*, 122.
14. Thompson, *Flash*, 57.
15. E. Ampofo-Duodu, "Symbolic Movements in Ghanaian Dances", *International Journal of African Dance* 1, no. 2 (1994): 29.
16. Ibid.
17. Gerald Jonas, *Dancing: The Pleasure, Power, and Art of Movement* (New York: Harry N. Abrahams, 1992), 107.
18. Ibid., 103.
19. Opoku, "Asante Dance Art".
20. Ampofo-Duodu, "Symbolic Movements", 34.
21. Placide Tempels, "Bantu Philosophy", in *African Philosophy: An Anthology*, ed. Emmanuel Chukwudi Eze (Malden, MA: Blackwell, 2001), 431.
22. Emmanuel Chukwudi Eze, "The Problem of Knowledge in 'Divination': The Example of Ifa", in *African Philosophy: An Anthology*, ed. Emmanuel Chukwudi Eze (Malden, MA: Blackwell, 2001), 173.
23. Harold Fromm, "The Hegemonic Form of Othering; or, the Academic's Burden", in *"Race", Writing, and Difference*, ed. Henry Louis Gates Jr and Kwame Anthony Appiah (Chicago: University of Chicago Press, 1986), 8.
24. Brown, *Systematic Remembering*, 214.
25. Richards, "Implications", 213.
26. Tempels, "Bantu Philosophy", 434.
27. Ibid., 430.
28. Michael Herzfeld, *Anthropology: Theoretical Practice in Culture and Society* (Malden, MA: Blackwell, 2001), 211.
29. Judith Lynne Hanna, "Movements toward Understanding Humans through the Anthropological Study of Dance", *Current Anthropology* 20, no. 2 (1979): 313–39.
30. Ni Yarte, conversation, 12 January 2005.
31. Victor Turner and Edith Turner, *Image and Pilgrimage in Christian Culture* (New York: Columbia University Press, 1978), 75.
32. Joseph Omoregbe, "African Philosophy: Today and Yesterday", in *African Philosophy: An Anthology*, ed. Emmanuel Chukwudi Eze (Malden, MA: Blackwell, 2001), 8.

33. Stuart Hall et al., *Culture, Media, Language: Working Papers in Cultural Studies, 1972–79* (London: Hutchinson, 1980), 235.

34. Hall, *Representation*, 3.

35. Lucy Burke, Tony Crowley and Alan Girvin, eds. *The Routledge Language and Cultural Theory Reader* (New York: Routledge, 2000), 419.

36. Geertz, *Interpretation*, 112.

37. Brandon, *Santeria*, 143.

References

Alleyne, Mervyn. *Roots of Jamaican Culture* London: Pluto, 1988.

Ampofo-Duodu, E. "Symbolic Movements in Ghanaian Dances". *International Journal of African Dance* 1, no. 2 (1994): 29–37.

Asante, Molefi Kete, and Kariamu Welsh Asante. "The Rhythms of Unity: A Bibliographic Essay in African Culture". In *African Culture: The Rhythms of Unity*, edited by Molefi Kete Asante and Kariamu Welsh Asante, 253–60. Trenton, NJ: Africa World Press, 1990.

Austin-Broos, Diane. J. *Jamaica Genesis: Religion and the Politics of Moral Orders*. Kingston: Ian Randle, 1997.

Beckles, Hilary, and Verene Shepherd. *Caribbean Slave Society and Economy: A Student Reader*. Kingston, Jamaica: Ian Randle, 1991.

Beckwith, Martha Warren. *Black Roadways: A Study of Jamaican Folk Life*. Chapel Hill, NC: University of North Carolina Press, 1929.

Beeman, William. "The Anthropology of Theatre and Spectacle". *Annual Review of Anthropology* 22 (1997): 369–93.

Behrend, Heike and Luig Ute, ed. *Spirit Possession: Modernity & Power in Africa*. Madison: University of Wisconsin Press, 2000.

Benítez-Rojo, Antonio. *The Repeating Island: The Caribbean and the Postmodern Perspective, Second Edition*, translated by James E. Maraniss. Durham, NC: Duke University Press, 1996.

Bilby, Kenneth. "Black Thoughts from the Caribbean". *New West Indian Guide* 57, nos. 3–4 (1983): 201–14.

Braithwaite, Kamau. *Contradictory Omens: Cultural Diversity and Integration in the Caribbean*. Mona: Savacou Publications, 1974.

Brandon, George. *Santeria from Africa to the New World: The Dead Sell Memories*. Bloomington: Indiana University Press, 1997.

Brodber, Erna. "Re-Engineering Blackspace". *Caribbean Quarterly* 43, nos. 1–2 (1997): 70–81.

Brown, Karen McCarthy. "Systematic Remembering, Systematic Forgetting: Ogou in Haiti". In *Africa's Ogun: Old World and New*, edited by Sandra T. Barnes, 204–25. Bloomington: Indiana University Press, 1997.

Browning, Barbara. *Samba: Resistance in Motion*. Bloomington: Indiana University Press, 1995.

Burke, Lucy, Tony Crowley and Alan Girvin, eds. *The Routledge Language and Cultural Theory Reader*. New York: Routledge, 2000.

Chevannes, Barry. *Rastafari and other African-Caribbean Worldviews*. 1995. Repr., New Brunswick, NJ: Rutgers University Press, 1998.

———. *Rastafari: Roots and Ideology*. Syracuse: Syracuse University Press, 1995.

———. "Revival and Black Struggle". *Savacou* 5 (1971): 27–39.

Climo, Jacob and Maria Cattel, eds. *Social Memory and History: Anthropological Perspectives*. New York: AltaMira Press, 2002.

Connerton, Paul. *How Societies Remember*. Cambridge: Cambridge University Press, 1989.

Courlander, Harold. *The Drum and the Hoe: Life and Lore of the Haitian People*. Berkeley: University of California Press, 1960.

Cudjoe, Seth. "The Techniques of Ewe Drumming and the Social Importance of Music in Africa." *Phylon* 14, no. 3 (1953): 280–91.

Curtin, Phillip. *Two Jamaicans: The Role of Ideas in a Tropical Colony, 1830–1865*. Cambridge, MA: Harvard University Press, 1955.

Dagan, Esther. *The Spirit's Dance in Africa: Evolution, Transformation, and Continuity in Sub-Sahara*. Westmount, QC, Canada: Galerie Amrad African Arts Publications, 1997.

Daniel, Yvonne. *Rumba: Dance and Social Change in Contemporary Cuba*. Bloomington: Indiana University Press, 1995.

Elkins, W. *Street Preachers, Faith Healers and Herb Doctors in Jamaica, 1890–1925*. New York: Revisionist Press, 1977.

Erskine, Noel, Leo. *Decolonizing Theology: A Caribbean Perspective*. Maryknoll, NY: Orbis, 1981.

Eze, Emmanuel Chukwudi. "The Problem of Knowledge in 'Divination': The Example of Ifa". In *African Philosophy: An Anthology*, edited by Emmanuel Chukwudi Eze, 173–75. Malden, MA: Blackwell, 2001.

Feld, Steven, and Keith H. Basso, eds. *Senses of Place*. Santa Fe, NM: School of American Research Press, 1996.

Floyd, Samuel A. Jr. *The Power of Black Music: Interpreting Its History from Africa to the United States*. New York: Oxford University Press, 1995.

Fra Ananael 138, and Sor. OchO/148. "The Seven African Gods". Manuscript, n.d.

Fraleigh, Sondora Horton, and Penelope Hanstein, eds. *Researching Dance: Evolving Modes of Inquiry*. Pittsburgh: University of Pittsburgh Press, 1999.

Fromm, Harold. "The Hegemonic Form of Othering; or, The Academic's Burden".

In *"Race", Writing, and Difference*, edited by Henry Louis Gates Jr and Kwame Anthony Appiah. Chicago: University of Chicago Press, 1986.

Fu-Kiau Bunseki, Kimbwandende Kia. *Tying the Spiritual Knot: African Cosmology of the Bântu-Kôngo: Principles of Life and Living*. Brooklyn, NY: Athelia Henrietta Press, 2001.

Geertz, Clifford. *The Interpretation of Cultures: Selected Essays*. New York: Basic Books, 1973.

Giles, Linda. "Spirit Possession and the Symbolic Construction of Swahili Society". In *Spirit Possession: Modernity and Power in Africa*, edited by Heike Behrend and Ute Luig, 142–64. Madison: University of Wisconsin Press, 1999.

Gordon, Shirley C. *Our Cause for His Glory: Christianisation and Emancipation in Jamaica*. Kingston: University of the West Indies Press, 1998.

Hall, Stuart. "Encoding, Decoding". In *The Cultural Studies Reader*, edited by Simon During, 97–112. New York: Routledge, 1993.

———. *Representation: Cultural Representations and Signifying Practices*. London: Sage, 1997.

Hall, Stuart, Dorothy Hobson, Andrew Lowe and Paul Willis. *Culture, Media, Language: Working Papers in Cultural Studies, 1972–79*. London: Hutchinson, 1980.

Hanna, Judith Lynne. "Movements toward Understanding Humans through the Anthropological Study of Dance". *Current Anthropology* 20, no. 2 (1979): 313–39.

Hebdige, Dick. "From Culture to Hegemony". In *The Cultural Studies Reader*, edited by Simon During, 357–67. New York: Routledge, 1993.

Heck, Thomas F. *Picturing Performance: The Iconography of the Performing Arts in Concept and Practice*. Rochester, NY: University of Rochester Press, 1999.

Henry, Paget. *Caliban's Reason: Introducing Afro-Caribbean Philosophy*. New York: Routledge, 2000.

Herskovits, Melville. J. *The Myth of the Negro Past*. Boston: Beacon Press, 1958.

Herzfeld, Michael. *Anthropology: Theoretical Practice in Culture and Society*. Malden, MA: Blackwell, 2001.

Highwater, Jamake. *Dance: Rituals of Experience*. Oxford: Oxford University Press, 1978.

Jary, David, and Julia Jary. *Collins Dictionary of Sociology*. Glasgow: HarperCollins, 1995.

Jonas, Gerald. *Dancing: The Pleasure, Power, and Art of Movement*. New York: Harry N. Abrahams, 1992.

Kaeppler, Adrienne L. "Dance in Anthropological Perspective". *Annual Review of Anthropology* 7 (1978): 31–49.

Kealiinohomoku, Joann W. "Theory and Methods for an Anthropological Study of Dance". PhD dissertation, Indiana University, 1976.

Kopytoff, Barbara. "The Development of Jamaican Maroon Ethnicity". *Caribbean Quarterly* 22, nos. 2–3 (1976): 33–48.

Lewin, Olive. *Rock It Come Over: The Folk Music of Jamaica*. Kingston: University of the West Indies Press, 2000.

Lohmann, Roger. "The Role of Dreams in Religious Enculturation Among the Asabano of Papua New Guinea". In *Dreams: A Reader on Religious, Rultural, and Psychological Dimensions of Dreaming*, edited by K. Bulkeley. New York: Palgrove, 2001.

Long, Edward. *History of Jamaica*. Volume 2, *Reflections on Its Situation, Settlements, Inhabitants, Climate, Products, Commerce, Laws, and Government*. London: Lowndes, 1974.

Makin, William J. *Caribbean Nights*. London: Robert Hale, 1939.

Mannheim, Bruce. "Iconicity". In *Key Terms in Language and Culture*, edited by Alessandro Duranti, 102–5. Oxford: Blackwell, 2001.

Markovitz, Irvin. *Power and Class in Africa*. Englewood Cliffs, NJ: Prentice Hall, 1977.

Martínez-Ruiz, Barbaro. "Mambo Comes from the Soul". In *Call and Response: Journeys in African Art*, edited by Sarah Adams, Barbaro Martínez-Ruiz, Robert Farris Thompson, Joanna Weber and Lyneise Williams, 79–120. New Haven, CT: Yale University Gallery Press, 2000.

Mbiti, John. *African Religions and Philosophy*. New York: Doubleday, 1969.

McCall, John. C. *Dancing Histories: Heuristic Ethnography with the Ohafia Igbo*. Ann Arbor, MI: University of Michigan Press, 2000.

McFee, Graham. *Understanding Dance*. New York: Routledge, 1992.

Mintz, Sidney. *Caribbean Transformations*. Chicago: Aldine Publishing, 1974.

Moore, Joseph. "Religion of Jamaican Negroes: A Study of Afro-Jamaican Acculturation". PhD dissertation, Northwestern University, 1953.

Murphy, Joseph. M. *Working the Spirit: Ceremonies of the African Diaspora*. Boston: Beacon Press, 1994.

Nettleford, Rex. "The Caribbean Creative Diversity: The Defining Point of the Region's History". Paper presented at Dancing across Disciplines, Intercultural Dance and Music Institute. Miami, Florida, 2000.

———. *Inward Stretch, Outward Reach*. London: Macmillan, 1993.

Nseedi, Lubasa. *The African Music–Song–Dance Trilogy (MSDT)*. Montreal, QC: Galerie Amrad African Arts Publications, 1997.

Olupona, Jacob K., ed. *African Spirituality: Forms, Meanings and Expressions*. New York: Crossroad, 2000.

Omoregbe, Joseph. "African Philosophy: Today and Yesterday". In *African Phi-*

losophy: An Anthology, edited by Emmanuel Chukwudi Eze, 3–8. Malden, MA: Blackwell, 2001.

Opoku, A.M. "Asante Dance Art and the Court". In *The Golden Stool: Studies of the Asante Center and Periphery*, edited by Enid Schildkrout, 192–99. Anthropological Papers of the American Museum of Natural History, vol. 65, part 1. New York: American Museum of Natural History, 1987.

———. "Aspects of Akan Worship", In *The Black Experience in Religion*, edited by C.E. Lincoln, 286–99. Garden City, NY: Anchor Press, 1974.

———. *Festivals of Ghana*. Accra: Ghana Publishing Corporation, 1970.

Parrinder, Geoffrey. *Encountering World Religions: Questions of Religious Truth*. Edinburgh: T. and T. Clark, 1987.

Patterson, Orlando. *The Sociology of Slavery: An Analysis of the Origins, Development and Structure of Negro Slave Society in Jamaica*. London: Granada, 1973.

P'Bitek, Okot. "The Sociality of Self". In *African Philosophy: An Anthology*, edited by Emmanuel Chukwudi Eze, 73–74. Malden, MA: Blackwell, 2001.

Peck, Phillip. "'Divination': A Way of Knowing?" In *African Philosophy: An Anthology*, edited by Emmanuel Chukwudi Eze, 171–72. Malden, MA: Blackwell, 2001.

Pitts, Walter. *Old Ship of Zion: The Afro-Baptist Ritual in the African Diaspora*. Oxford: Oxford University Press, 1993.

Ray, Benjamin. *African Religions: Symbols, Rituals and Community*. Englewood Cliffs, NJ: Prentice Hall, 1976.

———. "African Shrines as Channels of Communication". In *African Spirituality: Forms, Meanings and Expressions*, edited by Jacob K. Olupona, 26–37. New York: Crossroad, 2000.

Richards, Dona. "The Implications of African American Spirituality". In *African Culture*, edited by M.K. Asante and K.W. Asante, 207–31. Trenton, NJ: Africa World Press, 1990.

Sahlins, Marshall. *Islands of History*. Chicago: University of Chicago Press, 1985.

Schafer, D.L. "The Maroons of Jamaica and African Slave Rebellion in the Caribbean". PhD dissertation, University of Minnesota, 1973.

Schechner, Richard. *The Future of Ritual: Writings on Culture and Performance*. New York: Routledge, 1993.

Schuler, Monica. "Akan Slave Rebellion in the British Caribbean". *Savacou* 1 (1970): 8–31.

———. "Ethnic Slave Rebellions in the Caribbean and the Guianas". *Journal of Social History* 3, no. 4 (1970): 374–85.

———. "Myalism and the African Religious Tradition in Jamaica". In *Africa and the Caribbean: The Legacies of the Link*, edited by M. Crahan and F.W. Knight. Baltimore: Johns Hopkins University Press, 1979.

Seaga, Edward. "Revival Cults in Jamaica: Notes towards a Sociology of Religion". *Jamaica Journal* 3, no. 2 (1969): 1–13.

———. "River Maid, River Maid". *Jamaica Journal* 3, no. 2 (1969): 16–20.

Simpson, George Eaton. *Religious Cults of the Caribbean: Trinidad, Jamaica, and Haiti*. Puerto Rico: Institute of Caribbean Studies, University of Puerto Rico, 1970.

Sjørslev, Inger. "Possession and Syncretism: Spirits as Mediators in Modernity". In *Reinventing Religions: Syncretism and Transformation in Africa and the Americas*, edited by André Droogers and Sidney M. Greenfield, 131–44. New York: Rowman and Littlefield, 2001.

Sperber, Dan. *Rethinking Symbolism*, translated by Alice L. Morton. Cambridge: Cambridge University Press, 1974.

Stewart, Robert. J. *Religion and Society in Post-Emancipation Jamaica*. Knoxville: University of Tennessee Press, 1992.

Stoller, Paul. *Embodying Colonial Memories: Spirit Possession, Power and the Hauka in West Africa*. New York: Routledge, 1995.

Stuckey, Sterling. *Slave Culture: Nationalist Theory and the Foundations of Black America*. New York: Oxford University of Press, 1987.

Taylor, Patrick. *Nation Dance: Religion, Identity and Cultural Difference in the Caribbean*. Kingston: Ian Randle, 2001.

Tempels, Placide. "Bantu Philosophy". In *African Philosophy: An Anthology*, edited by Emmanuel Chukwudi Eze, 429–34. Malden, MA: Blackwell, 2001.

Thompson Drewal, Margaret. *Yoruba Ritual: Performers, Play, Agency*. Bloomington: Indiana University Press, 1992.

Thompson, Robert Farris. *Flash of the Spirit: African and Afro-American Art and Philosophy*. New York: Random House, 1983.

Torres, Arlene and Norman E. Whitten Jr, eds. *Blackness in Latin America and the Caribbean: Social Dynamics and Cultural Transformations*. Bloomington: Indiana University Press, 1998.

Turner, Victor. *The Anthropology of Performance*. New York: PAJ Publications, 1988.

———. *The Forest of Symbols: Aspects of Ndembu Ritual*. Ithaca: Cornell University Press, 1967.

———. *The Ritual Process: Structure and Anti-structure*. Hawthorne, NY: Aldine De Gruyter, 1969.

Turner, Victor, and Edith Turner. *Image and Pilgrimage in Christian Culture*. New York: Columbia University Press, 1978.

Vansina, Jan. *Oral Tradition as History*. Madison: University of Wisconsin Press, 1985.

Waddell, Hope. *Twenty-Nine Years in the West Indies and Central Africa: A Review of Missionary Work and Adventure, 1829–1858.* London: Nelson, 1970.

Wedenoja, William A. "Religion and Adaptation in Rural Jamaica". PhD dissertation, University of California, San Diego, 1963.

Welsh Asante, Kariamu, ed. *African Dance: An Artistic, Historical and Philosophical Inquiry.* Trenton, NJ: African World Press, 1998.

———. *Zimbabwe Dance: Rhythmic Forces, Ancestral Voices – An Aesthetic Analysis.* Trenton, NJ: Africa World Press, 2000.

Williams, D. "Traditional Danced Spaces: Concepts of Deixis and the Staging of Traditional Dance". *International Journal of African Dance* 1, no. 2 (1994): 8–20.

Williams, Joseph J. *Jamaican Witchcraft.* Westport, CT: Greenwood, 1934.

———. *The Maroons of Jamaica.* Boston: Boston College Press, 1938.

Young, Robert. J. C. *Colonial Desire: Hybridity in Theory, Culture and Race.* London: Routledge, 1995.

Zahan, Dominique. "Some Reflections on African Spirituality". In *African Spirituality: Forms, Meanings and Expressions*, edited by Jacob K. Olupona, 3–25. New York: Crossroad, 2000.

Zips, Werner. *Black Rebels: African-Caribbean Freedom Fighters in Jamaica*, translated by Shelley L. Frisch. Kingston: Ian Randle, 1999.

Interviews and Personal Communication with Author

Asante Griot, 12 November 2003, Kumasi, Ghana.
Bishop Bansy, 29 January 2002, Gethsemane United Holy Church, St Catherine.
Sylvia Bates, 8 March 2002, Watt Town, St Ann.
Bishop Blake, 8 August 2001, Watt Town, St Ann.
Bishop Boonie, 1 March 2001, Sacred Heart Church, Olympic Gardens, Kingston.
Bishop Bourne, 3 March 2001, Sacred Heart Church, Olympic Gardens, Kingston.
———, 18 September 2001, Molynes Gardens, Kingston.
———, 19th March 2002; 6th March 2003 Sacred Heart Church
Pastor Brown, 26 July 2003, Sacred Heart Church, Olympic Gardens, Kingston.
Mother Campbell, 26 June 2003, Sacred Heart Church, Olympic Gardens, Kingston.
Brother Clive, 8 March 2002, Watt Town, St Ann.
Pastor Queenie Brown, 29 January 2002, University of the West Indies, Mona Campus, Kingston.
———, September 2002, University of the West Indies, Mona Campus, Kingston.
———, 11 October 2002, University of the West Indies, Mona Campus, Kingston.
Elder Dacosta, 3 March 1977
Mother Nora Dawnes, 6 December 2005, Georges Plain, Westmoreland.

Queen Esther, 9 April 2001, Sacred Heart Church, Olympic Gardens, Kingston.

Reverend Foster, 8 March 2002, Watt Town, St Ann.

Pastor Tony Gordon, 8 March 2002, Watt Town, St Ann.

Esther Grant, 23 October 2002, August Town, Kingston.

Bishop Guthrie, 2 March, 2006, Watt Town.

Bishop Hill, 26 January 2002, Gethsemane United Holy Church, St Catherine.

——, 19 January 2003, Gethsemane United Holy Church, St Catherine.

Vineyard Mother Humes: 17 September 2001, Sacred Heart Church, Kingston.

——, 21 January 2003, Sacred Heart Heart Church, Kingston.

Mother Yvonne Hyatt, 25 September 2001, Hyatt's Drug Store, Downtown Kingston.

Bishop Jack, 8 March 2002, Watt Town, St Ann.

Edgar Linton, 6 March 2003, Watt Town, St Ann.

Lilieth Morrison, 21 January 2003, University of the West Indies, Mona Campus, Kingston.

Pastor Morrison, 3 March 2001, Watt Town, St Ann.

——, 22 January 2003, Sacred Heart Church, Olympic Gardens, Kingston.

Ni Yarte, 10–15 January 2005, Dance of Our Ancestors Conference, Temple University, Philadelphia.

Pastor Payne, 8 March 2002, Watt Town, St Ann.

Bishop Reid, 28 January 2002, Sacred Heart Church, Olympic Gardens, Kingston.

——, 19 June 2002, Sacred Heart Church, Olympic Gardens, Kingston.

——, 22 May 2003, Sacred Heart Church, Olympic Gardens, Kingston.

Mother Richards, 19 May 2002, Sacred Heart Church, Olympic Gardens, Kingston.

——, 8 March 2003, St Andrew.

Bishop Rose, 7 June 2001, Watt Town, St Ann.

Daddy Rudd, 15 November 2001, August Town, Kingston.

——, 1 July 2002, August Town, Kingston.

——, 23 October 2002, August Town, Kingston.

Mother Simon, 7 June 2001, Watt Town, St Ann.

Evangelist Millicent Vassell, 8 March 2002, Watt Town, St Ann.

Sister Vickie, 23 January 2003, Waltham Park Road, Kingston.

Welsh Asante Kariamu, 5 July 2004, Jamaica Cultural Development Commission workshop, Shortwood Teachers' College, Kingston.

Index

Page numbers in italics refer to photographs.